Creating Smart-er Cities

Drawing upon the smart experiences of "world class" cities in N. America, Canada and Europe, this book provides the evidence to show how entrepreneurship-based and market dependent representations of knowledge production are now being replaced by a community of policy makers, academic leaders, corporate strategists and growth management alliances with the potential to liberate cities from the stagnation they have previously been locked into. In particular, it will show how such market-based representations of knowledge production are now being replaced by a community of policy makers and academic leaders with:

- the corporate strategies and growth management alliances capable of reaching beyond the idea of "creative slack";
- a notion of innovation which allows cities to reach beyond the idea of creative slack and be "smarter" in generating the intellectual capital that is needed to meet the efficiency requirements of wealth creation;
- the "wealth of intellect" also needed for cities to not only be economically innovative and culturally creative, but smarter in drawing upon the enterprise required for industry and government to open-up, reflexively absorb and discursively shape these strategic alliances;
- the "creative" means for such a participatory system of governance to be smarter when not only liberating cities from the stagnation they have previously been locked into, but in freeing them up to promote the type of civic renewal smarter cities also pave the way for.

Bringing together the critical insights of papers drawn from a collection of leading international experts on the transition to smart cities, this book proposes to do what has recently been asked of those responsible for *Creating Smart-er Cities*. That is: to assemble the definitional components, critical insights and institutional means by which to get beyond the all too often self-congratulatory tone cities strike when claiming to be smarter.

This book was published as a special issue of the *Journal of Urban Technology*.

Mark Deakin is Professor of Built Environment in the School of Engineering and Built Environment, Edinburgh Napier University. He is also Head of the Centre for Sustainable Communities in the Institute for Sustainable Construction, at Edinburgh Napier University. His research focuses on sustainable urban development, intelligent cities, smart cities and communities.

Creating Smart-er Cities

Edited by
Mark Deakin

Routledge
Taylor & Francis Group

LONDON AND NEW YORK

First published 2013
by Routledge
2 Park Square, Milton Park, Abingdon, Oxfordshire OX14 4RN
Simultaneously published in the USA and Canada
by Routledge
711 Third Avenue, New York, NY 10017

First issued in paperback 2014

Routledge is an imprint of the Taylor & Francis Group, an informa business

© 2013 The Society of Urban Technology

This book is a reproduction of the *Journal of Urban Technology*, vol. 18, issue 2. The Publisher requests to those authors who may be citing this book to state, also, the bibliographical details of the special issue on which the book was based.

All rights reserved. No part of this book may be reprinted or reproduced or utilised in any form or by any electronic, mechanical, or other means, now known or hereafter invented, including photocopying and recording, or in any information storage or retrieval system, without permission in writing from the publishers.

Trademark notice: Product or corporate names may be trademarks or registered trademarks, and are used only for identification and explanation without intent to infringe.

British Library Cataloguing in Publication Data
A catalogue record for this book is available from the British Library

ISBN 978-0-415-62802-0 (hbk)
ISBN 978-1-138-79844-1 (pbk)

Typeset in Times New Roman
by Taylor & Francis Books

Publisher's Note
The publisher would like to make readers aware that the chapters in this book may be
referred to as articles as they are identical to the articles published in the special issue. The publisher accepts responsibility for any inconsistencies that may have arisen in the course of preparing this volume for print.

Contents

Citation Information   vii
Notes on Contributors   viii

1. Creating Smart-er Cities: An Overview
   Sam Allwinkle and Peter Cruickshank   1

2. The IntelCities Community of Practice: The Capacity-Building, Co-Design, Evaluation, and Monitoring of E-Government Services
   Mark Deakin, Patrizia Lombardi, and Ian Cooper   17

3. The Business Models and Information Architectures of Smart Cities
   George Kuk and Marijn Janssen   39

4. The Triple-Helix Model of Smart Cities: A Neo-Evolutionary Perspective
   Loet Leydesdorff and Mark Deakin   53

5. Smart Cities in Europe
   Andrea Caragliu, Chiara Del Bo, and Peter Nijkamp   65

6. SCRAN: The Network
   Peter Cruickshank   83

Index   99

Citation Information

The chapters in this book were originally published in the *Journal of Urban Technology*, volume 18, issue 2 (April 2011). When citing this material, please use the original page numbering for each article, as follows:

Chapter 1
Creating Smart-er Cities: An Overview
Sam Allwinkle and Peter Cruickshank
Journal of Urban Technology, volume 18, issue 2 (April 2011) pp. 1-16

Chapter 2
The IntelCities Community of Practice: The Capacity-Building, Co-Design, Evaluation, and Monitoring of E-Government Services
Mark Deakin, Patrizia Lombardi, and Ian Cooper
Journal of Urban Technology, volume 18, issue 2 (April 2011) pp. 17-38

Chapter 3
The Business Models and Information Architectures of Smart Cities
George Kuk and Marijn Janssen
Journal of Urban Technology, volume 18, issue 2 (April 2011) pp. 39-52

Chapter 4
The Triple-Helix Model of Smart Cities: A Neo-Evolutionary Perspective
Loet Leydesdorff and Mark Deakin
Journal of Urban Technology, volume 18, issue 2 (April 2011) pp. 53-64

Chapter 5
Smart Cities in Europe
Andrea Caragliu, Chiara Del Bo, and Peter Nijkamp
Journal of Urban Technology, volume 18, issue 2 (April 2011) pp. 65-82

Chapter 6
SCRAN: The Network
Peter Cruickshank
Journal of Urban Technology, volume 18, issue 2 (April 2011) pp. 83-98

Notes on Contributors

Sam Allwinkle is a Professor in the Institute of Sustainable Construction at Edinburgh Napier University.

Andrea Caragliu is a Research Fellow at the Politecnico of Milano.

Ian Cooper is a partner at Eclipse Research Consultants in Cambridge, United Kingdom.

Peter Cruickshank is a Research Fellow in the School of Computing at Edinburgh Napier University.

Mark Deakin is a Professor in the School of Engineering and Built Environment at Edinburgh Napier University.

Chiara Del Bo is a Research Fellow at Università degli Studi di Milano.

Marijn Janssen is an Associate Professor in the Faculty of Technology, Policy, and Management at Delft University.

George Kuk is an Associate Professor in the Business School at Nottingham University.

Loet Leydesdorff is a Professor in the Department of Communication Science at the University of Amsterdam.

Patrizia Lombardi is a Professor in the Dipartimento Casa-Città at Politecnico of Torino.

Peter Nijkamp is a Professor in the VU University, Amsterdam.

Creating Smart-er Cities: An Overview

Sam Allwinkle and Peter Cruickshank

ABSTRACT *The following offers an overview of what it means for cities to be "smart." It draws the supporting definitions and critical insights into smart cities from a series of papers presented at the 2009 Trans-national Conference on Creating Smart(er) Cities. What the papers all have in common is their desire to overcome the all too often self-congratulatory nature of the claims cities make to be smart and their over-reliance on a distinctively entrepreneurial route to smart cities. Individually, they serve to highlight the major challenges cities face in their drive to become smart. Collectively they begin to uncover what it means for cities to be smart. Together the papers offer an alternative route to smart cities laid down by those advocating a more neo-liberal roadmap, rooted in a critically aware knowledge-base and more realistic understanding of what it means for cities to be smart(er).*

Introduction

Smart city forerunners like San Diego, San Francisco, Ottawa, Brisbane, Amsterdam, Kyoto, and Bangalore are all now setting a trend for others to follow. Other cities now keen to follow in their wake and become "smart" include: Southampton, Manchester, Newcastle, Edinburgh, Edmonton, Vancouver, and Montreal.

This overview of Smart Cities is drawn from six papers presented at the Creating Smart(er) Cities Conference, organized in accordance with the European Commission's Interreg North Sea IVB Program and hosted by Edinburgh Napier University, March 2009.[1] They have been collected in this issue because collectively they begin to do what Hollands (2008) has asked of Smart Cities: to provide the definitional components, critical insights, and institutional means by which to get beyond the all too often self-congratulatory tone cities strike when claiming to be smart.

Taking Hollands' (2008) statement about the "unspoken assumption" surrounding the "self-declaratory" nature of smart cities as the point of departure, this paper reflects upon the anxieties currently surrounding their development. In particular, it investigates the suggestion that such developments have more to do with cities meeting the corporate needs of marketing campaigns than the social intelligence required for them to be smart. Working on the assumption that any attempt to overcome such anxieties has cities shift their attention away from the needs of the market and towards the intelligence required for them to be smart, the paper begins to set out a critical evaluation of smart cities.

Will the Real Smart City Please Stand Up

In his 2008 article, "Will the Real Smart City Please Stand Up?" Richard Hollands argues that cities all too often claim to be smart, but do not define what this means, or offer any evidence to support such proclamations. The all too often "self-congratulatory" tone cities strike when making such claims does not seem to sit well with Hollands (2008). For while images of the digital city, intelligent city, high-tech district, and neighborhoods of smart communities abound, they all fail to convey what it means to be "smart" and why it is important for cities to be defined in such terms.

In Hollands' (2008) opinion, the validity of any city's claim to be smart has to be based on something more than its use of information and communication technologies (ICTs). Hollands (2008) makes this observation because cities all over the world are beginning to claim that they are "smart" because they employ ICTs in their operations. Such smart city forerunners as San Diego, San Francisco, Ottawa, Brisbane, Amsterdam, Kyoto, and Bangalore set a trend for others to follow. The other cities keen to follow in their wake and become smart include Southampton, Edinburgh, Manchester, Vancouver, and Montreal. It appears the rush to become a smart city has begun to gather apace and as a consequence, pressure is now growing for cities to become even smarter.

Two such efforts identified on the Smart City Thinking website are examples of this trend <www.smartcitythinking.com>: Amsterdam Smart City (a business, government, and community partnership pursuing a project portfolio focused on energy saving in the form of "Sustainable-Work, Living, Mobility, and Public Spaces") and the City of Edinburgh Council's Smart City Vision (a project that focuses on e-government infrastructure to improve the performance and delivery of public services while supporting access and participation). Manchester's current move to develop a landscape of connected monitoring devices supporting impact mapping and program design across social, environmental, and economic domains constitutes another example.

Novel infrastructures that serve as platforms or facilitators of new beneficial behavior forms the backbone of a number of Smart City programs. ICT infrastructures, underpinned by a new generation of mobile technologies, connected devices, network platforms, and associated software also hold a central position in this landscape.

IBM's high-profile campaign on smart cities also goes someway to acknowledge this pressure for cities to become smarter. As the company's promotional materials state (IBM, 2010):

> Technological advances [now] allow cities to be "instrumented," facilitating the collection of more data points than ever before, which enables cities to measure and influence more aspects of their operations. Cities are increasingly "interconnected," allowing the free flow of information from one discrete system to another, which increases the efficiency of the overall infrastructure....To [meet] these challenges and provide sustainable prosperity for citizens and businesses, cities must become "smarter" and use new technologies to transform their systems to optimize the use of finite resources.

The "Self-Congratulatory" Nature of Smart City Claims

Hollands' (2008) anxiety about the "self-congratulatory" nature of the claims cities make to be smart tends to hark back to the image-building and city marketing campaigns of the 1990s and the competition this sparked among cities. Hollands' (2008) fear of using such an ill-defined notion to spearhead yet another marketing campaign lies in the tendency that such strategies have to be almost exclusively entrepreneurial in outlook, undermining the more collaborative and consensus-building aspirations of the networking paradigm.

Hollands (2008) asks us to be aware that if left to be entrepreneurial, there is a strong chance that smart cities will develop in a way that he believes will be too neo-conservative and insufficiently progressive.

From the Intelligent to Smart City

Hollands advocates that cities should follow a less neo-conservative and more neo-liberal pathway to "smart-er" cities. Here he relies on Komninos's (2002; 2008) work on the intelligent city that the author says has four main components:

- the application of a wide range of electronic and digital technologies to communities and cities
- the use of information technologies to transform life and work within a region
- the embedding of such ICTs in the city
- the territorialization of such practices in a way that brings ICTs and people together so as to enhance the innovation, learning, knowledge, and problem-solving that the technologies offer.

This much needed definition of what it means for intelligent cities to be smart is in turn used by Hollands (2008:306) to clear the way for a vision of cities that are smart-er because they are: "...territories with a high capacity for learning and innovation, which is built in to the creativity of their population, their institutions of knowledge production, and their digital infrastructure for communication."

For Hollands the key elements of this definition relate to the use of networked infrastructures as a means to enable social, environmental, economic, and cultural development. While this involves the use of a wide range of infrastructures including transport, business services, housing, and a range of public and independent services (including leisure and lifestyle services), it is the ICTs of these developments that are of critical importance because they "undergird" all of these networks and single them out as the common denominator lying at the core of the smart-er city.

The ICTs lying at the core of the networks include: mobile and land line phones, satellite TVs, computer networks, electronic commerce, and Internet services. Hollands sees them as important because he considers the intelligence such infrastructures embed as the main driving force behind the development of smart-er cities, those capable of sustaining social, environmental, and cultural progress.

Towards Smart-er Cities

While Hollands (2008:315) argues that by definition "smart-er cities" are "wired" cities, he notes that this cannot be the sole defining criterion because: "progressive(ly) smart[er] cities must seriously start with people and the human capital side of the equation, rather than blindly believing that IT itself can automatically transform and improve cities."

For Hollands, the critical factor in any successful community, enterprise, or venture is its people and how they interact. This is because for Hollands the most important thing about information technology is not its capacity to create smart cities, but the possibility it offers for them to be an integral part of a much wider social, economic, and cultural development. That is to say, ICTs can serve as communications that are smart for the way they allow cities to empower and educate their citizens so that they can become members of society capable of engaging in a debate about their own environment. This, it is stressed, in turn, is only possible when the community of people undergoing the process of socialization are able to:

> create a real shift in the balance of power between the use of information technology by business, government, communities, and ordinary people who live in cities, as well as seek to balance economic growth with sustainability. ...In a word, the "real" smart city might use IT to enhance democratic debates about the kind of city it wants to be and what kind of city people want to live in (Hollands, 2008:316).

To achieve this, Hollands suggests, those cities that really want to be smarter will have to "take much greater risks with technology, devolve power, tackle inequalities, and redefine what they mean by 'smart' itself, if they want to retain such a lofty title" (316).

Some Immediate Reflections

While Hollands' image of what it means to be smart-er tends to start with the worst-case nightmare scenario of a city dominated by the entrepreneurial values of the elite few, it is clear this vision of a somewhat unintelligent, neo-conservative, and less than liberal representation is soon swept aside by a more progressive alternative. An alternative, which, in this instance, uses information technology, not to shore-up the entrepreneurial values of the city, but in a way which is smart in the sense they are used to "undergird" their social, communal, and environmental qualities. As a "best-dream" scenario, this works well to allay any fears that may linger about the purpose of smart cities and ways in which they should be put to work.

As with all such visions, there are, however, some inconsistencies and omissions in the narrative and storylines in the reworked version of what is being represented, i.e., the smart-er city. These relate to both the legacy of smart cities and the more contemporary issues underlying their development.

Hollands' representation of the "smart city legacy" is, perhaps, just a little too "fast and furious," in the sense that his retrospective probably relies less on the notion of "informational cities" advanced by the likes of Castells (1996) or Graham and Marvin (1996; 2001) and more on Mitchell's (1995; 1999; 2001; 2003) accounts of what it means for the technologies of such infrastructures "to work smarter not harder!" For while Castells and Graham and Marvin draw attention to the information technologies of the so-called critical infrastructures (water and drainage, energy and the like), it is Mitchell (1995; 1999; 2001; 2003), who first deployed them in the Smart City laboratory at MIT and sought to sketch out how informational technologies make it possible to network the intelligence of smart cities.

The Smart Card Legacy

Hollands labels Southampton the first smart city because it was the first to develop a portal capable of supporting smart card applications for public transport, recreation, and leisure-related transactions. For this initiative, promoted under the triple-helix model of university, industry (the tele-communications sector) and government, was the first to develop smart-card software that gave access to a variety of services distributed across the public and independent sectors. It was also the first city to develop software capable of supporting the transactional-based logic of multi-application management architectures that allowed services to be added or removed as part of the card's dynamic user environment.

The administration of the card scheme involved the processing of personal data that had to be done in compliance with U.K. and EU data protection legislation. Both the university sector and the industrial sector were keenly aware of the privacy issues arising from any association with government-sponsored card schemes. To comply with the legislation, each smart card was given a unique identifier that could be used by all service applications to identify the user, and when transaction information was sent to the data warehouse, this unique identifier was "one-way" encrypted. This meant the unique identifier was scrambled, so transaction information could not be traced back to any user whose personal data was held in the warehouse. However, even though the information held in the data warehouse was stored anonymously, it was still considered to be "personal data," because it was possible to match it with information in other databases.

Under the legislation, if service providers wished to share personal data under their control, they had to be able to specify the purpose and follow a data-sharing protocol. However, where multiple applications were provided by the same data controller, the data collected from these applications could be used in the course of any legitimate interest. This may include cross matching and trend analysis, where this directly relates to a notified purpose.

It is the ability this portal has to deal with multiple transactions simultaneously and as "bundles of services" in a real-time environment that attracted so much attention from those cities seeking to be smart in supporting the development of these kinds of e-government services. This entailed cities shifting attention away from the e-commerce challenges of the enterprise architecture and transaction-based business logic underlying the development of e-government services and towards what Halpern (2005) sees as being something much smarter—the social capital of networked communities.

Towards the Smart Community

Halpern (2005:508) speaks of social capital being composed of, "a network; a cluster of norms, rules, values, and expectations; and sanctions." Here communities form networks and co-operate with one another in accordance with a set of norms, rules, values, and expectations that link members of the community, bridging the divisions that exist in civic society.

Halpern understands ICTs to be forms of social capital and lists several prerequisites for the development of networked communities. These are examined in terms of the potential networked communities, virtual organizations, and managed learning environments that develop the ecological integrity and equity of regeneration as part of the on-going process of democratic renewal needed for socially inclusive decision making. He writes:

> While the vast majority of community ICT experiments have to date not met the conditions above [the ecological integrity, equity, democratic renewal, needs and requirements]....ICT networks may have great potential to boost local social capital, provided they are geographically "intelligent," that is, are smart enough to connect you directly to your neighbors; are built around natural communities; and facilitate the collection of collective knowledge. They have the potential to connect the work-poor and work-rich (Halpern, 2005:509-510).

The Methodological Twist

The methodological twist in Halpern's (2005) discussions on "geographically intelligent settlements" lies in the fact this examination of networks, virtual organizations, and managed learning environments precedes that of the planning, development, and design of planned villages and neighborhoods. Networks, virtual organizations, and managed learning environments, whose "geography of intelligent settlements," are in turn seen as providing the info-structures for communities to collaborate and build consensus on the development of high-tech and digitally enabled platforms that offer the informational basis for the planning, development, and design in question. That type of planning, development, and design goes a long way to strengthen the norms, rules, and values of settlements by providing the citizens of these communities with a platform to bridge the gap between the "work-poor and work-rich" by providing them with the means to not only build a platform capable of tying the "work-rich" and the "work-poor" together in communities but within settlements strong enough and sufficiently resilient to carry the environmental weight and economic expectation (vis-à-vis, ecological integrity and equity) of their ongoing regeneration.

Networks, Innovation, and Creative Partnerships

So where are these ICT-enabled networks that boost the norms, rules, and values of local social capital? These networks are geographically "intelligent," that is, smarter because they are sufficiently innovative to connect "villagers" directly to "neighbors" and do this by virtue of being based on creative partnerships that are built around "natural" communities. These natural communities facilitate the generation of collective knowledge that can be drawn upon to meet the expectations of their on-going generation.

Contrary to popular belief, such urban regeneration programs are not limited to the United Kingdom, but can be found throughout Europe. Examples of the two-way interactive communications evident in the smart-card experiment initiated by Southampton can also be found in Edinburgh, Helsinki, Glasgow, and Dublin (Deakin, et al., 2005; Deakin and Allwinkle, 2006). The following offers a very brief account of the networks, innovation, and creative partnerships underlying the villages and neighborhoods of the geographically intelligent and smart community regeneration programs underway in Edinburgh as part of the city's Social Inclusion Partnerships (SIPs). It examines the city's smart regeneration programs for the Wester Hailes and Craigmillar communities (Deakin and

Allwinkle, 2007). An account of the urban regeneration partnerships governing the planning, development, and design of Wester Hailes and Craigmillar can be found in Hastings (1996), Carley (1996), Carley and Kirk (1998), and Carley et al.'s (2000) report on such developments. The development of these networks and innovations are also reported by Slack (2000), Malina (2001; 2002) Malina and MacIntosh (2004), and McWilliams et al. (2004). Malina and Ball (2004) have also reported on the development of social capital emerging from these innovations and have addressed the question of whether the villages and neighborhoods emerging are not just geographically "intelligent," but are "smart-er" in the sense their communities connect "villagers" to their "neighbors."

The following shall cut across these reports and draw attention to the creative partnership(s) emerging from the planning, development, and design of the villages and neighborhoods of the communities in question. Similar developments underway in Helsinki are reported on by Sotarauta (2001), Kostiainen and Sotarauta (2003), and Sotarauta and Srinivas (2006). Dabinett (2005) also reports on the situation emerging in Glasgow and Dublin.

myEdinburgh.org

As an ICT-enabled network, *myEdinburgh.org* is innovative because it gets beyond the user-centered environment of the smart-card legacy by providing an information portal and community grid for learning (CGfL). This particular information portal provides citizens with the user-friendly tools for communities to access learning opportunities. Within this environment, the CGfL provides the infrastructure needed for citizens to learn about the planning, development, and design of their cities and engage in local decisions made about the promotion of urban villages and neighborhoods as sustainable communities under the city's urban regeneration strategy.

The Edinburgh Learning Partnership, composed of representatives from local government agencies, the education sector, voluntary groups, and private-sector businesses, provides the creative basis for the networking and innovation the portal and grid offers access to. As a city-wide venture, the collaboration seeks to encourage and facilitate initiatives that are creative in widening access to and increasing participation in learning activities, particularly those which target the disadvantaged. The key aims of the partnership can be summarized as follows:

- to provide citizens with ICT "taster" sessions in local, accessible venues, specifically targeting citizens identified as "digitally excluded" (for example, citizens living in Edinburgh's SIPs)
- to support community and voluntary organizations in the procurement, use, and development of ICTs, including training staff to access and maintain the information portal
- to develop a Community Grid for Learning (CGfL)
- to use that grid for learning as a way to build capacity and engage citizens in local decision making
- to draw upon this knowledge as a means for communities to participate in the planning, development, design, and layout of villages and neighborhoods by "visioning" the regeneration program and petitioning the key gatekeepers required to meet the material realities of such an inclusive and participatory modernization.

The E-Learning, Knowledge Transfer, and Capacity-Building Technologies

The resulting e-learning platform makes it possible for the online service applications being demonstrated to be integrated with the knowledge transfer and capacity-building technologies needed to meet the interoperability requirements of such developments. This allows citizens, communities, and organizations to collaborate and build consensus about the competencies, skills, and training needed for the development of the online services required to support urban regeneration. (See Figure 1.)

Together, the networks, innovation, and creativity of these partnerships are responsible for organizing the development of those technologies, skills, and training exercises that make it possible to engage citizens in this process and show how active participation is both intelligent and smart because it develops the social capital setting the normative standards and rule-based logic of those civic values governing the ecological integrity and equity of democratic renewal.

What the Papers All Have in Common

For many, there is no difference between intelligent and smart cities. Many academics and leading consultancies are of the same opinion when it comes to the question of what is meant by the terms "intelligent" and "smart." This is particularly so for the advocates of intelligent cities who use the terms intelligent and smart cities to mean the same thing. Komninos (2002; 2008) offers just such an example of this, as does IBM.

For the authors of the papers brought together in this focus issue, however, this is not the case. They believe there is a difference between the terms. For

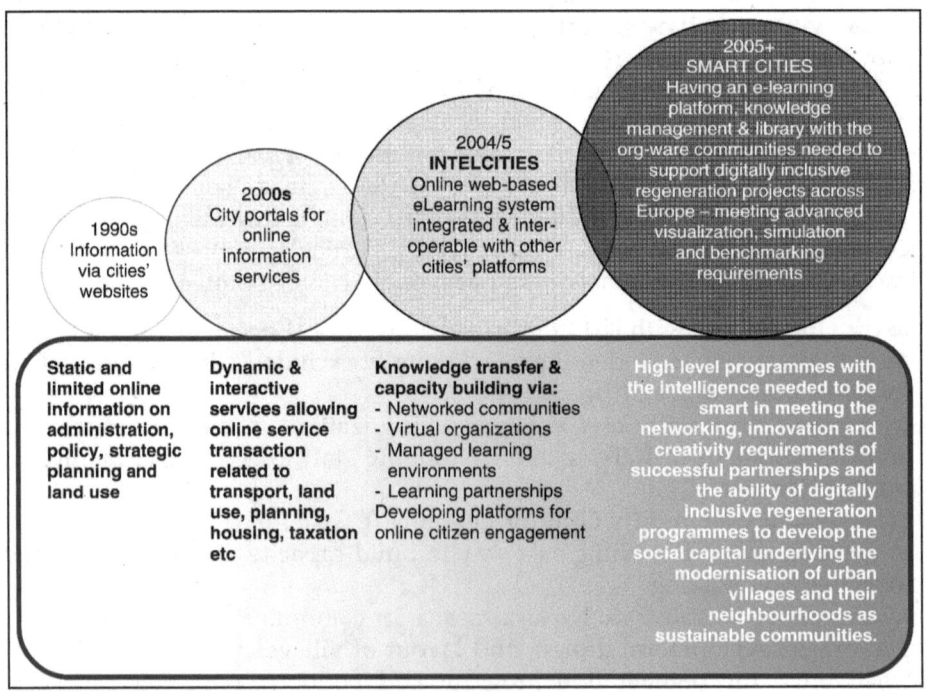

Figure 1. The development of digitally inclusive regeneration programs
Source: Deakin and Allwinkle (2007)

these authors, intelligence is not so much about the computational power, memory, data-bases, information systems, or knowledge-transfer capabilities of cities, but the means such innovations offer them to learn from the application of these technologies.

The thing to bear in mind here is that for smart cities the capacities that intelligent cities have sought to develop over the past twenty years or so become the technical platform for their application across a host of service-related domains. For it is here and at this stage of development that the point of emphasis and intervention begins to shift from innovation to application, from the back-office to front-line services, and in policy terms, the emphasis also shifts from the corporate to the civic, from the market to the community, and from the bureaucratic administration of the economy to a liberal democratic governance.

This shift from innovation to application is what current representations of intelligent cities tend to miss. Focusing almost exclusively on innovation, they limit their terms of reference to service promotion. In particular, they limit it to the promotion of services and their bureaucratic administration, rather than application. Furthermore, their bureaucratic administration supports the market rather than serving as a platform for the community, and as an exercise in liberal democratic governance, or civitas. Developed in this way, the platform is not simply economic, but is also social, environmental, and cultural.

These papers represent an attempt to shift the emphasis from the promotion and administration of services to the liberal democratic governance of their applications. In doing so, they follow others (Hollands, 2008; Komninos, 2008; Deakin and Allwinkle, 2007; Halpern, 2005) who study the current state of innovation within cities. Some papers examine how government is brought into an area dominated by industry and the university. Others try to determine how the institutionalization of this three-way partnership can break with the marketing, promotion, and administration of the past and set the stage for using the technologies of the intelligent city to improve the quality of life in communities through the socially inclusive use of environmental and culturally-related service applications.

Together the papers advocate a more neo-liberal roadmap, rooted in a critically aware knowledge-base and more realistic understanding of what it means for cities to be smart(er). In this respect, they offer a language, a syntax, and a vocabulary by which to understand the emerging policy debate on smart cities.

The Papers

While the desire to overcome the all too often self-congratulatory tone of cities claiming to be smart is what all the papers in this issue have in common, individually they serve to highlight the major challenges cities face attempting to become "smart."

While this paper has reviewed the policy debate on smart cities, the second paper, written by Mark Deakin, Patrizia Lombardi, and Ian Cooper, develops the notion of an intelligent city as the provider of electronically-enhanced services. It identifies how the growing interest in the notion of intelligent cities has led universities to explore the possibilities of using "communities of practice" (CoPs) as a means of drawing upon the industrial knowledge-base such organizations offer in developing integrated models of e-government (eGov) services. It reports on the attempt made by a consortium of leading European cities (led by Manchester) to use the intelligence that CoPs offer as the means by which to work "smarter" in developing integrated models of e-government services.

Composed of researchers, computer engineers, informational managers, and public-sector service providers, the IntelCities CoP has worked to develop an integrated model of eGov services and to support the actions taken by cities to host them on platforms with sufficient intelligence to meet the e-learning needs, knowledge-transfer requirements, and capacity-building commitments of socially-inclusive and participatory urban regeneration programs.

As an exercise in CoP development, this organization is particularly successful because the intelligence it has sought to embed in cities and integrate within their platforms of eGov services is inter-organizational, networked, virtual, and managed as part of a highly-distributed, web-based learning environment. Composed of open-source software groups, experts, and lay people, the CoP is unique in the sense its network provides an example of a virtual organization set up to manage the learning needs and knowledge requirements of a technological platform. As such it:

- offers the means to meet the learning needs, knowledge-transfer requirements, and capacity-building commitments of the organization
- co-designs them as a set of services that are socially inclusive and participatory and that allow users to learn about the availability of the services, how to access them, and the opportunities they offer to become engaged in meeting the knowledge-transfer requirements and capacity-building commitments of their urban regeneration programs
- allows for the monitoring and evaluation of these actions.

As the authors make clear, it is the e-learning platform that makes it possible for the online services under development to be integrated with the knowledge-transfer and capacity-building technologies that are needed for this CoP to work as a shared enterprise, one that allows organizations to collaborate and build consensus on the competencies, skills, and training needed for the required online developments.

Together, the networks, innovation, and creativity of the partnerships responsible for organizing the development of these technologies, skills, and training exercises make it possible to engage citizens and show how the active participation of communities is both intelligent and smart. This turns attention to what is termed the e-Topia demonstrator developed to illustrate the functionality of the semantically-rich eGov services in question. This term is borrowed from Mitchell's (1999; 2001) account of intelligent cities as e-topias and as organizations that are: "SMART," lean, mean, green software systems, driven by networked communities that are virtual (see, Deakin and Allwinkle, 2007). Those are the organizational characteristics that are built on the learning needs, knowledge-management requirements, and digital libraries of the electronically-enhanced government services that are made available on the e-City platform as a pool of integrated eGovernment services.

As this paper goes some length to highlight, the extensive nature of these developments means questions about the enterprise architecture and business models of such ventures become critical to any such integration. This is the particular "smart cities" challenge the third paper in the issue focuses on. For as George Kuk and Marijn Janssen point out, many local governments in the Netherlands are currently reforming their online services by exploring new web-based models. Deliberate or not, many of them are following the integrating logic of the IntelCities CoP and moving their enterprise architecture onto "a full-service provider (FSP) business model." This model facilitates "user-centric" interaction through direct information and service provisioning and involves collaboration among a number of departments, including previously disjointed organizations, to provide all services in a one-stop shop (e.g., Janssen et al., 2008). However, despite the intuitive appeal of the FSP model, the authors of this paper explain how the model might not suit all types of public agencies and is likely to require enterprise-wide technological changes.

The fourth paper by Loet Leydesdorff and Mark Deakin turns the table on these technical accounts of smart cities and examines the developments from the neo-evolutionary perspective of the triple helix. Leydesdorff and Deakin argue that the urban technologies of cities can be modeled as network densities among the dynamics of: organized knowledge production, the economics of wealth creation, and governance of civil society. These interactions, they explain, can be expected to generate spaces where knowledge can be produced and exploited to create added value. The authors suggest the dynamics at play in this development can be facilitated by the pervasive technologies of information-based communications (ICTs) currently being exploited to generate the notion of "creative cities" (Landry, 2008) and as the knowledge base of "intelligent cities" (Komninos, 2008). They go further and assert that these technologies are now being asked to work even "smart-er," not just in the way they make it possible for cities to be intelligent in generating capital and creating wealth, but in co-evolving with these developments and creating environments that produce knowledge in innovation systems.

Going against the grain, Leydesdorff and Deakin suggest that the reinvention of cities as "smart" currently taking place during an "urban renaissance," cannot be defined as a top-level "trans-disciplinary" issue without a considerable amount of cultural reconstruction at the bottom. They argue that the highly distributed character of this reconstruction has not yet been given the consideration it demands. For accounts of this cultural reconstruction tend to reify the global perspective and fail to appreciate the meta-stable dynamics of such communications as innovations systematically worked out as the informational content of social processes operating at the local level.

The triple helix, they stress, is important to understand for the communication codes it offers up as a means of obtaining knowledge of what this renaissance means for cities. For what the triple helix does is help distinguish the codes of communication that operate within CoPs from the translation mechanisms that allow their institutions to work out what this means. This neo-evolutionary analysis guides them towards the intellectual capital of such creativity by focusing attention on those dimensions of corporate management that make it possible for urban regeneration programs to function as meta-stabilizing mechanisms underpinning civil society's integration of cities into the governance of their emerging innovation systems (Deakin and Allwinkle, 2007; Deakin, 2008; 2009a and b).

This knowledge-based reconstruction must be political and economic as well as cultural if urban regeneration programs are to function as systems of innovation that respond to the "creative destruction" of the global and the "reflexive reconstruction" of the local. They explain that the "creative reflexivity" of this meta-stabilization is far from "symbolic," or of merely representational significance insofar as it generates the critical reinforcement needed to communicate the democratic values civil society requires to govern over any such "programmatic" integration of cities into their emerging innovation systems.

While methodological in substance, the matters that Leydesdorff and Deakin draw attention to should not be seen as offering an alternative perspective on the intelligence of smart cities. For in developing the critical insight needed to get inside such developments, it offers a mirror image of the matters also of utmost concern to the previous papers. For the critical distinction between them is methodological and lies in the reluctance of those adopting the triple-helix model to rely solely on technical accounts as the means to explain such developments.

Not content with these technical accounts, triple-helix models seek to explain such development in organizational terms. That is, in terms of what it means for cities to be smart and for organizations to exploit the potential their CoPs have to be innovative in developing integrative e-government service models. Those e-government service models have the enterprise architecture and business models capable of building the capacity to co-design services and for that reason, this FSP can, in turn, be made subject to monitoring and evaluation.

In the fifth paper, Andrea Caragliu, Chiara Del Bo, and Peter Nijkamp provide the evidence to support the assertions underlying many of the previous articles' arguments regarding the critical relationship between the intellectual capital and wealth creation of knowledge production and the development of e-government services by smart cities. In line with the triple helix model, it begins with the assumption that the intellectual capital of wealth creation depends not only on the endowment of hard infrastructure ("physical capital"), but also, and increasingly more so, on the "social capital" of the city's knowledge-base.

Referring to the concept of smart cities, the authors suggest this has emerged as a means to highlight the important role that the intellectual capital of ICTs now plays in governing the wealth that is created from the regeneration of cities. Given the growing significance of the concept, the paper analyzes the all too often elusive definition of "smart cities" and goes on to analyze the geography of smart cities in Europe.

This original and unique analysis provides the statistical basis to examine the relationship between intellectual capital, wealth creation, and the development of e-government services of smart cities across Europe. Using data drawn from the EC's Urban Audit statistics, the paper attempts to analyze the factors determining the development of smart cities. It highlights the presence of a "creative class," with the intellectual capital to access high-quality urban assets, educational opportunities, and government services underlying the development of smart cities. More significantly, it identifies the intellectual capital allowing access to such assets, opportunities, and services, which are all positively correlated with the creation of wealth. These findings are important because they start to build the evidence-base to support the previously unchallenged assumption about the existence of a positive relationship between the pool of intellectual capital, the stock of wealth created, and the governance of the knowledge economy.

Given the wide-ranging and generic nature of these findings, the paper then outlines how this can be used to bootstrap the technology of innovation systems and exploit their intellectual capital to generate wealth. The outcome of this examination is then used to formulate a new strategic agenda for governing the development of smart cities across Europe.

Using the triple-helix model to focus on the organizational means of smart cities also has the advantage of uncovering the true magnitude of what is at stake with such developments. In the final paper, Peter Cruickshank attempts to capture just this. He draws upon the representation of smart cities, intelligent enterprise architectures, and business models underlying the triple helix outlined in earlier papers and provides an example of how such understandings can be put to good use as a knowledge base for universities, industry, and government to draw upon. Starting with the triple helix of SCRAN's methodology, Cruickshank draws attention to how the communication needs and technical requirements of the three-way partnership can be met.

In setting out how SCRAN is doing this, Cruickshank configures the triple helix of the network and sets out the "step-wise" logic of the partnership's knowledge base. He explains the networking of the university and industrial sectors involved in the Smart Cities venture and then details how the knowledge base created from that network can be used as a learning platform for the partnership to take the eGov service development program full-circle.

Cruickshank argues that the three-way partnership of the university, industry, and government captures the science and technology around which the triple-helix model for regional development turns. This explains SCRAN's particular take on the triple helix and serves as a means of drawing attention to the science and technology underpinning the strategic research funded by the European Union and the United Kingdom. That funding supports the innovative and creative use of ICTs as a platform for the electronic enhancement of government services. This in turn serves to highlight the innovative and creative capacities of the Smart Cities partnership and what can perhaps best be referred to as a statement of the academic network's e-government services capability. From here, the organizational means needed for business to meet these standards and those also required by government to meet their expectations are explored in terms of the partnership's ability to begin co-designing the (inter)regional development of e-government services and do this in a way that allows the transnational dimensions of this program to be mainstreamed across the North Sea.

This representation of the triple-helix model goes some way to uncover the scientific and technical capacity of the research-based services this particular academic network offers the Smart Cities partnership. Cruickshank says that SCRAN offers the Smart Cities partnership a platform of ICTs supporting the business communities' (inter)regional development of e-government services. This is accomplished through:

- the policies, plans, programs and projects underlying the (inter)regional development of electronically-enhanced government services
- the legacy of experiential learning that the academic network brings to the project
- an understanding of the e-government services supported by the platform of ICTs, including reduced bureaucracy, back-office re-organization, and customer focus
- the e-government services it is possible for the network to pool together and manage as a common resource shared with the industrial and university sectors
- the individual and collective competencies that support the regional development of the electronically-enhanced services required by government.

Cruickshank proposes that organizations like SCRAN focus attention on the underlying technical issues and in particular, those supporting the partnership's enterprise architecture and business modeling. From here it is proposed SCRAN's attention should turn to the co-design of the customized and multi-channeled use of the e-government services that the Smart Cities partnership proposes to develop.

The mediawiki knowledge infrastructure chosen to support this process is set out in terms of how this social technology can be used to answer questions raised about Smart Cities. The paper suggest this shift towards a triple-helix perspective among policy makers, researchers, and members of the business community marks a major step forward in knowledge production. This is because in such institutional settings regional innovation systems are seen to offer the opportunity for triple-helix models to replace so-called "mode 2" notions of policy, i.e., research and business. That is, cities should replace hierarchies and networks with CoPs that offer the intelligence needed for cities to be smart in constructing regional advantage and to do so by understanding that community-based learning of smart cities is the creative force underlying this shift in the knowledge-base of university, industry, and government alike.

Note

1. The Conference was organized as part of the methodological inquiries supporting the development of the Smart Cities Regional Academic Network (SCRAN) funded under the European Commission's Interreg North Sea IVB Program (for further information see: <http://www.smartcities.info>).

Bibliography

M. Carley, "Partnership and Statutory Local Governance in a Devolved Scotland," *International Journal of Public Sector Management* 19:3 (1996) 250–260.

M. Carley and K. Kirk, *Sustainable by 2020? A Strategic Approach to Urban Regeneration for Britain's Cities* (Bristol: Policy Press, 1998).

M. Carley, A. Chapman, A. Hastings, K. Kirk, and R. Young, *Urban Regeneration Through Partnership: A Study in Nine Urban Regions in England, Scotland, and Wales* (Bristol: Policy Press, 2000).

M. Castells, *Rise of the Network Society: The Information Age* (Cambridge: Blackwell, 1996).

G. Dabinett, "Competing in the Information Age: Urban Regeneration and Economic Development Practices," *Journal of Urban Technology* 12:3 (2005) 19–38.

M. Deakin, "The IntelCities Community of Practice: The eGov Services Model for Socially-Inclusive and Participatory Urban Regeneration Programs," in C. Reddick, ed., *A Handbook of Research on Strategies for Local e-Government Adoption and Implementation: Comparative Studies* (Hershey: IGI Global, 2009a).

M. Deakin, "Towards a Community-Based Approach to Sustainable Urban Regeneration," *Journal of Urban Technology* 16:1 (2009b) 91–112.

M. Deakin and S. Allwinkle, "The IntelCities Community of Practice: The e-Learning Platform, Knowledge Management Systems, and Digital Library for Semantically-Interoperable e-Governance Services," *International Journal of Knowledge, Culture, and Change in Organizations* 6:2 (2006) 155–162.

M. Deakin and S. Allwinkle, "Urban Regeneration and Sustainable Communities: The Role Networks, Innovation, and Creativity in Building Successful Partnerships," *Journal of Urban Technology* 14:1 (2007) 77–91.

M. Deakin, S. Allwinkle, F. Campbell, and K. Van Isacker, "The IntelCities e-Learning Platform, Knowledge Management System, and Digital Library," in M. Cunningham and P. Cunningham, eds., *Innovation and the Knowledge Economy: Issues, Applications, Case Studies* (Amsterdam: IOS Press, 2005).

S. Graham and S. Marvin, *Splintering Urbanism* (London: Routledge, 2001).

S. Graham and S. Marvin, *Telecommunications and the City* (London: Routledge, 1996).

D. Halpern, *Social Capital* (Bristol: Policy Press, 2005).

A. Hastings, "Unraveling the Process of Partnership in Urban Regeneration Policy," *Urban Studies* 33:2 (1996) 253–268.

R. Hollands, "Will the Real Smart City Stand Up? Creative, Progressive, or Just Entrepreneurial?," *City* 12:3 (2008) 302–320.

IBM, *Smart Cities* (2010), <www-935.ibm.com/services/us/gbs/bus/html/smarter-cities.html> Accessed July 13, 2011.

M. Janssen, G. Kuk, and R.W. Wagenaar, "A Survey of Web-based Business Models for e-Government in the Netherlands," *Government Information Quarterly* 25:2 (2008) 202–220.

N. Komninos, *Intelligent Cities and Globalization of Innovation Networks* (London: Taylor & Francis, 2008).

N. Komninos, *Intelligent Cities: Innovation, Knowledge Systems, and Digital Spaces* (London: Spon Press, 2002).

J. Kostiainen and M. Sotarauta, "Great Leap or Long March to Knowledge Economy: Institutions, Actors, and Resources in the Development of Tampere, Finland," *European Planning Studies* 10:5 (2003) 415–438.

C. Landry, *The Creative City* (London: Earthscan, 2008).

A. Malina, "Community Networks and Perception of Civic Value," *Communications* 27 (2002) 211–234.

A. Malina, "Electronic Community Networks," *Journal of Community Work and Development* 1:2 (2001) 67–83.

A. Malina and I. Ball, "ICTs and Community: Some Suggestions for Further Research in Scotland," *Journal of Community Infomatics* 1:3 (2005) 66–83.

A. Malina and A. MacIntosh, "Bridging the Digital Divide: The Development in Scotland," in Ari-veikko-Anttroiko *et al.*, eds., *eTransformation in Governance* (London: Idea Group Publishing, 2004).

M. McWilliams, C. Johnstone, and G. Mooney, "Urban Policy in New Scotland: The Role of Social Inclusion Partnerships," *Space and Polity* 8:3 (2004) 309–319.

W. Mitchell, *City of Bits: Space, Place, and the Infobahn* (Cambridge Massachusetts: MIT Press, 1995).

W. Mitchell, *e-Topia: Urban Life, Jim but not as You Know It* (Cambridge, Massachusetts: MIT Press, 1999).

W. Mitchell, "Equitable Access to an On-line World," in D. Schon, B. Sanyal, and W. Mitchell, eds., *High Technology and Low-Income Communities* (Cambridge Massachusetts: MIT Press, 2001).

W. Mitchell, *Me ++: The Cyborg-Self and the Networked City* (Cambridge Massachusetts: MIT Press, 2003).

S. Slack, "The Dialectics of Place and Space: On Community in the Information Age," *New Media and Society* 2:3 (2000) 313–334.

Smart City Thinking: Digital Urban Futures (2010) <www.smartcitythinking.com> Accessed July 13, 2011.

M. Sotarauta, "Network Management and Information Systems in Promotion of Urban Economic Development: Some Reflections from CityWeb of Tampere," *European Planning Studies* 6 (2001) 693–706.

M. Sotarauta and S. Srinivas, "Co-Evolutionary Policy Processes: Understanding Innovative Economies and Future Resilience," *Futures* 38:3 (2006) 312–336.

The IntelCities Community of Practice: The Capacity-Building, Co-Design, Evaluation, and Monitoring of E-Government Services

Mark Deakin, Patrizia Lombardi, and Ian Cooper

ABSTRACT *The paper examines the IntelCities Community of Practice (CoP) supporting the development of the organization's capacity-building, co-design, monitoring, and evaluation of e-government services. It begins by outlining the IntelCities CoP and goes on to set out the integrated model of electronically enhanced government (e-government) services developed by the CoP to build the capacity to co-design, monitor, and evaluate the IntelCities' e-Learning platform, knowledge-management system, and digital library. The paper goes on to examine the information technology (IT) underlying this set of semantically interoperable e-government services supporting the crime, safety, and security initiatives of socially-inclusive and participatory urban regeneration programs.*

Introduction

The notion of the intelligent city as the provider of electronically-enhanced services has been popular for more than a decade (Graham and Marvin, 1996; Mitchell, 2000). In response to this growing interest in the notion of intelligent cities, researchers have begun to explore the possibilities of using the IntelCities Community of Practice (CoPs)[1] as a means to get beyond current state-of-the-art solutions and use the potential such organizations offer to develop integrated models of e-government (eGov) services (Curwell, et al., 2005; Lombardi and Curwell, 2005). What follows reports on the outcomes of one such exploration and reviews the attempt made by a consortium of leading European cities to use the intelligence that CoPs offer as the organizational means by which to get beyond current state-of-the art solutions. The CoP in question is that developed under the IntelCities Project and is known as the IntelCities CoP.

IntelCities was a research project pooling the experience of electronically-enhanced service developments across Europe. The project was led by Manchester City Council (UK) and the City of Siena (Italy) and brought together 36 research groups, 18 cities, and 20 ICT companies (including Nokia and CISCO). The project formed part of the European Union's Sixth Framework Program, with a €6.8m budget from the EU's Information Society Technologies Program. The project aimed to create a new and innovative set of interoperable, e-government services providing information on all aspects of city life over the web. By providing these services, IntelCities aimed to:

- improve the quality of information available to assist with the planning, development, and design of electronically-enhanced services
- support the everyday needs of citizens and business, by providing 24-hour access to transactional city services
- develop efficient city management systems by integrating services across local authorities, regional and national government agencies, and their utility providers
- enable decision making to be more inclusive and allow both citizens and businesses to play a far more participative role in the design of such integrated service delivery.

The IntelCities Community of Practice

The IntelCities CoP is composed of research institutes, information, communication, and technology (ICT) companies, and cities, all collaborating with one another and reaching consensus on how to develop integrated models of eGov services. The IntelCities CoP has worked to develop an integrated model of eGov services and support the actions taken to host them on platforms (in this instance something known as the eCity platform) with sufficient intelligence to meet the e-learning needs, knowledge transfer requirements, and capacity-building commitments of socially-inclusive and participatory urban regeneration programs (Deakin and Allwinkle, 2006).

As an exercise in CoP development, the organization is particularly successful for the reason the intelligence it has sought to embed in cities and integrate within their platforms of eGov services is inter-organizational, networked, virtual, and managed as part of a highly-distributed web-based learning environment. If we quickly review the legacy of CoPs in organizational studies, the value of developing such a learning environment should become clear.

Literature on CoPs

The literature on CoPs reveals many different kinds of situated practices, all of them displaying quite varied processes of learning and knowledge gathered around distinct forms of social interaction. Wegner's (1998; 2000) studies of CoPs, for example, detail the ways that insurance claim processors and other such occupational groups learn to be effective in their jobs. Orr (1996) also studies the importance of CoPs amongst photocopier repair technicians. Osterlund (1996) studies are of CoPs as learning organizations that cut across craft, occupational, and professional divisions and transfer knowledge among them. The collective representation of CoPs in the literature suggests such organizations have the characteristics outlined in Table 1.

Taking this representation of CoPs as a starting point for their examination, Amin and Roberts (2008) suggest there are four distinct types of inter-organizational learning and knowledge transfer: craft, professional, creative and virtual.[2] As Amin and Roberts (2008) point out, until recently it has been assumed that virtual organizations are not capable of promoting learning and transferring knowledge. Although, as it becomes easier to communicate with "distant others" in real time and in increasingly rich ways, the resulting proliferation of online learning means interest is now centering on how the knowledge dynamics of such organizations differ from CoPs that are dependant on social familiarity and direct engagement to sustain their mutual relationships (Ellis et al., 2004; Johnson, 2001).

Table 1: Key characteristics of a community of practice

- sustained mutual relationships
- ways of engaging in doing things together
- the rapid flow of information and the propagation of innovation
- absence of introductory preambles, as if conversations and interactions were merely the continuation of an ongoing process
- very quick setup of a problem to be discussed
- substantial overlap in participants' descriptions of who belongs
- knowing what others know, what they can do, and how they can contribute to an enterprise
- mutually defining identities
- the ability to assess the appropriateness of actions and products
- specific tools, representations, and other artifacts
- local lore, shared stories, inside jokes, knowing laughter
- jargon and shortcuts to communication as well as the ease of producing new ones
- certain styles recognized as displaying membership
- a shared discourse reflecting a certain perspective on the world

Source: Compiled from Wenger (1998)

Two Types of Online Interaction

As Amin and Roberts (2008) acknowledge, there are now two types of online interaction that merit close attention as spaces where CoPs engage in learning and get involved in knowledge generation. The first type consists of innovation-seeking projects that can involve a large number of participants while the second type consists of relatively closed interest groups that face specific problems and are consciously organized as platforms for learning about and gaining a knowledge of, how to build the capacity to include "distant others" as participants in such projects.

Amin and Roberts note that open-source software groups provide a good example of the first type of CoP. Typically, they involve short-lived projects that make source code freely available to technical experts who are motivated by the challenge of solving a difficult programming problem. Successful projects of this kind are those guided by shared notions of the problem and by a core group of highly motivated experts who associate with one another to learn about the subject and transfer the knowledge generated to distant others.

More recently, however, we have seen a rapid rise in the development of the second type of CoP. These are established explicitly by professionals, experts, or lay people to advance knowledge. Typically, they involve experts interested in developing and exchanging best practices, or lay people wishing to not only learn about, or transfer knowledge about a given subject, but build the capacity for this to take place via electronically-mediated communication.

Here a CoP is seen to emerge once the technologies for the virtual organization are available and success is seen to emerge from the ability such platforms have to transfer knowledge. Furthermore, it is also stressed that with this type of CoPs, the technology available to support the development of such a virtual learning organization is something that has to be managed. Josefsson (2005) suggests that these organizations should be managed in accordance with a "netiquette," where semantically-rich language is used to develop a culture of engagement, replete with humor, empathy, kindness, tact, and support. In this way virtual learning organizations are seen to replicate the rich texture of social interaction normally associated with CoPs marked by high levels of inter-personal trust and reciprocity, or collaborations built around strong professional or occupational ties.

Defining Features of the IntelCities CoP

Made up of both open-source software groups, experts and lay people, the IntelCities CoP is unique in the sense its network provides an example of a virtual organization set up to manage the learning needs and knowledge requirements of a technological platform. The Community of Practice (CoP) developed by the IntelCities Project was designed to:

- offer the means to meet the learning needs, knowledge transfer requirements, and capacity building commitments of the organization
- be socially inclusive and participatory and allow users to learn about the availability of services, the ways to access them, and the opportunities they offer everyone to meet the knowledge transfer requirements and capacity-building commitments of their urban regeneration programs
- allow for the monitoring and evaluation of such actions.

There are three features that define the IntelCities CoP that give it meaning and a sense of purpose. These can be paraphrased as: building the capacity for a shared enterprise, co-designing their online services, and both monitoring and evaluating those services.

Building the Capacity for a Shared Enterprise

It is the CoP's e-learning platform that makes it possible for the online services under development to be integrated with the knowledge-transfer and capacity-building technologies that are needed for this to work as a shared enterprise. This is because this platform alone makes it possible for the citizens, communities, and organizations in question to collaborate with one another and build consensus on the competencies, skills, and training needed for the development of the required online services.

Such a shared enterprise is made possible because:

- the ICT-enabled networks underpinning all of this are innovative in developing an e-learning platform based on open-source technologies that are interoperable across online services
- this high-tech, digitally enabled network allows for the planning, development, and design of the online service requirements
- such services allow the applications under consideration to be integrated with the e-learning, knowledge-transfer, and capacity-building technologies supporting the regeneration programs under review
- such technologies allow citizens and communities to collaborate and build consensus on the competencies, skills, and training needed for the online services under development to support the quintessentially civic values of this regeneration program
- together these networks, innovations, and partnerships create the trust needed to engage citizens and show how the active participation of communities in digitally-inclusive regeneration is both intelligent and smart in developing the social capital—norms, rules, and civic values—of the ecological integrity and equity underlying this modernization
- the ecological integrity and equity of the democratic renewal take the form of consultations and deliberations in government and citizen-led decision making that engages citizens as members of a community who participate in the governance of this ongoing modernization.

The resulting platform supports the distribution, storage, and retrieval of learning materials, skill packages, and training materials needed for the engagement and participation that bridges the digital divides.

Co-Designing On-Line Services

The IntelCities CoP has sought to co-design eGov services by overcoming the limitations of a customer-focused approach and by supplementing this with a more user-centric strategy. (Lombardi, et al., 2009). Here collaboration is based not only on notions of either a sovereign consumer or customer, but on the consensus built among those citizens who participate in such a process of co-design (Berger et al., 2005). Here the informational and transactional logic of mass customization is seen as being supplemented with a process of participatory co-design that is more democratic in the way it goes about meeting personal preferences. This strategy advocates that citizens participate in the co-design of products not as customers, but as users of the services and through their involvement in workshops that promote the authoring, self-documentation, and recording of their creative experiences. Here the objective of the co-design strategy is not the mass customization of products, or the personalization of service provision, but the forging of a collective process that allows citizens to collaborate with one another as a community of subjects who are sufficiently empowered to govern such developments (Nicklaus, et al., 2008; Binder, et al., 2008).

Monitoring and Evaluating

For those involved in the "co-designing" of eGov services, it is not so much their customization, or the multi-channel access that is associated with this, but the outcomes of the process that is subject to monitoring and evaluation. This is because for this group of stakeholders, co-design provides a basic measure of value and demonstrates, not whether a service can be trans-acted, but if this is useful.

As the defining features of the IntelCities CoP, the aforementioned align with the characteristics previously highlighted by Amin and Roberts (2008) and set out in Table 1. Table 2 underlines the importance of these as characteristics and adds another six that have been exploited by the network to develop a virtual learning organization capable of bridging the gap that exists between the two types of virtual CoPs described by Amin and Roberts (2008). The extra characteristics are those needed to span the divide between the transactional-based logic of the first type and the user-centric reasoning that the second adopts towards the co-design of eGov services.

In line with current definitions of CoPs as shared enterprises, the additional features clearly highlight these particular qualities and reflect their importance, but in addition to this, they underline the technical, rational, and social purpose of the virtual organization in question. This suggests that in building the capacity to co-design eGov services, it is not possible for intelligent cities to develop as either the first or second type of CoPs and this is because they have to be technical and social in equal measures. In other words, they have to rest on the transactional-based logic of (innovative-seeking) customization and the user-centric reasoning of (knowledge-generating) eGov services in equal measures.

The following examination of the IntelCities CoP will to a large extent reflect this position. It will begin by examining the capacity that the CoP has built to

Table 2: Defining characteristics of the IntelCities CoP

- sustained mutual relationships
- ways of engaging and in doing things together
- the rapid flow of information and the propagation of innovation
- absence of introductory preambles, as if conversations and interactions were merely the continuation of an ongoing process
- very quick setup of a problem to be discussed
- substantial overlap in participants' descriptions of who belongs
- knowing what others know, what they can do, and how they can contribute to an enterprise
- a shared discourse reflecting a certain perspective on the world
- shared enterprise between research institutes, ICT companies, and cities
- joint venture commitment to product development
- building the capacity for ICTs to be used as a means of bridging the digital divide
- the co-design of services
- shared commitment to social-inclusion and participatory urban regeneration programs as a means to close the gap between the information-rich and the information-poor
- support for the modernization of local government service provision using technological platforms
- consensus-based decision making, consultative and deliberative in nature
- monitoring and evaluating

co-design an integrated model of eGov services and IT underlying the eCity platform developed as an intelligent solution for the virtual organization's learning needs and knowledge-transfer requirements. The examination shall then reflect on the search for intelligent city solutions in terms of the step-wise logic adopted to meet the challenge the learning needs and knowledge-transfer requirements that such virtual organizations pose. From here, the e-learning platform, knowledge-management system, and digital library developed for such purposes shall be outlined. Having done this, attention shall turn to the innovative features of the platform, management system, and library and the semantically interoperable qualities of the learning, knowledge, and repository services this offers. Then the examination turns towards a review of how the learning, knowledge-management system, and digital library services now available as eGov services are integrated into the eCity platform and made available over the web.

This turns attention to what is termed the eTopia demonstrator developed to illustrate the functionality of the semantically-rich eGov services in question. This term is borrowed from Mitchell's (2000) account of intelligent cities as e-topias and as organizations that are "SMART," lean, mean, green software systems, driven by networked communities that are virtual (Deakin and Allwinkle, 2007; Deakin, 2007). Those organizational characteristics that the authors would add are built on the learning needs, knowledge-management requirements, and digital libraries of electronically-enhanced government services and that are available on the eCity platform as a pool of integrated eGov services.

The Integrated Model of E-Government Services

Figure 1 outlines the integrated eGov services model developed by the CoP. At the front-end there are a range of eGov services under development, highlighted as social inclusion, participation, and regeneration and shown in terms of the middleware integrating them between the front-end presentation tier and the back-office core interoperability and infrastructure service layer of the eCity platform. This also illustrates the services located in the back-office and the

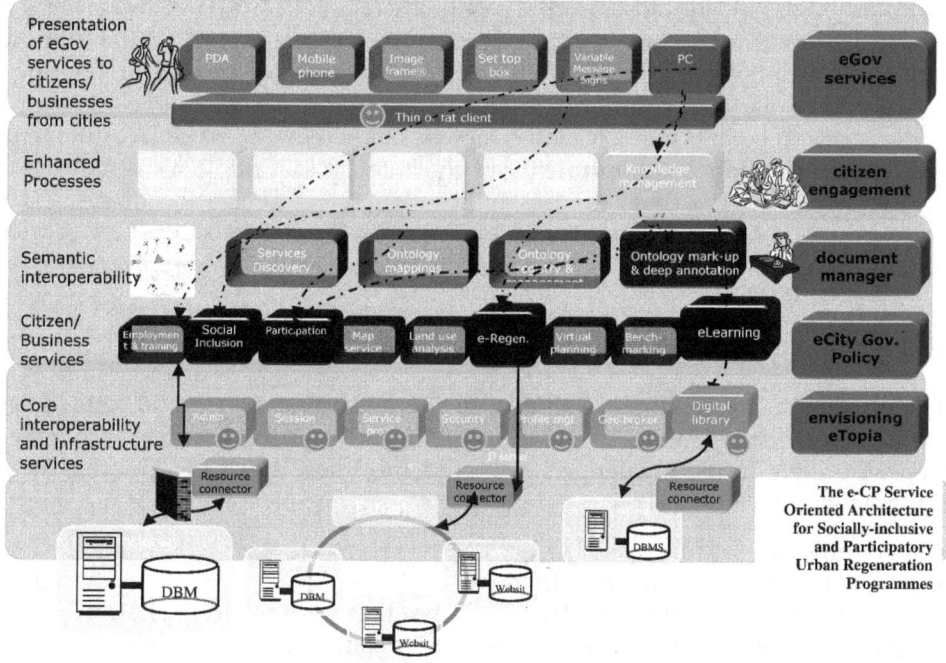

Figure 1. Integrated eGov services model

relationship this develops between the organization's e-learning platform, its knowledge-management system, and the digital library.

The figure shows that it is the middleware of the eCity platform that integrates the front-end delivery of government services to citizens with the back-office business functions. Figure 1 also shows that it is the middleware that in turn provides the opportunity for the e-learning platform, the knowledge-management system, and the digital library that make up the back-office functions and become an integral part of the eCity platform, supporting the pool of eGov services which are available for citizens to access at the front-end. The integration of these services into the middleware and the use of this middleware as the eCity platform supporting the presentation of eGov services to citizens at the front-end, is the goal of the IntelCities CoP.

The main challenge for the IntelCities CoP has been that of finding a solution that has the intelligence cities need to make the information technology (IT) underpinning of eGov services extensible, flexible, and capacious enough to carry existing local government legacy systems. The Services Oriented Architecture (SOA) of the enterprise-wide business model adopted as the joint venture vehicle for the "intelligent solution" meets this challenge by offering the IntelCities CoP a distributed, web-based, and extendable access system. This intelligence in turn offers cities the opportunity to build a web-service-enabled platform of eGov services, with Extensible Markup Language (XML) IT utilization and Simple Object Access Protocol (SOAP) communication.

An important element in the initial system design relates to the use of the Unique Modeling Language (UML) and Rational Unified Process (RUP) methodology used for developing the integrated model of electronically-enhanced government (eGov) services. This allows for the development of complex "N-tiered" systems and the possibility of cities hosting eGov services on e-Learning platforms, knowledge-management systems, and digital libraries utilizing the intelligence such IT offers. This has the advantage of offering a homogenous platform solution supporting the development of specific service applications meeting the e-learning needs, knowledge-transfer requirements, and capacity-building commitments of the IntelCities CoP. It also manages to do this while leaving open the possibility for this customization of services to be co-designed by other organizations not yet integrated into the eGov services model and eCity platform.

The Search for an Intelligent Solution

The search for an intelligent solution to the e-learning needs and knowledge-management requirements of the eCity platform has progressed by applying a step-wise logic to the challenge it poses to the IntelCities CoP. This has taken the following form:

- surveying user learning needs
- analyzing the knowledge requirements
- reviewing learning and knowledge services that leading city portals provide
- benchmarking existing e-learning platforms against the user's knowledge transfer and capacity-building requirements
- selecting the e-learning platform able to meet these requirements and developing it as a knowledge-management system supported by a digital library
- integrating the aforesaid into the IntelCities middleware as a platform of eGov services delivered to citizens at the front-end.

Following this step-wise logic has meant focusing attention on the underlying pedagogical issues—the competencies, skills, and training requirements of IntelCities. The next step involved a review of the learning services that leading city portals offer as legacy systems and benchmarking of the e-learning platforms these systems are based upon against the knowledge-transfer and capacity-building requirements of the IntelCities CoP. Here the learning services of five leading city portals were reviewed (Deakin et al., 2004; Campbell and Deakin, 2005). These included the learning services provided on the city portals of: Edinburgh, Dublin, Glasgow (Drumchapel), Helsinki (Arabianranta and Munala), and Reykjavic (Garoabaer). The review found:

- the city portals provide learning services for citizens
- the portals provide citizens with a community grid for learning
- much of the data available to the community is informative, telling citizens about learning opportunities in their neighborhoods and providing links to the service providers
- while being used by up to 10 percent of the population and offering free e-mail and storage, most of the services provided by the city portals were insufficiently engaging for citizens to use them as grids for communities to base their development of learning partnerships on.

The review found these e-learning platforms to be primarily informational, and while they offer inter-active learning opportunities, they were insufficiently developed to meet the knowledge transfer requirements of the IntelCities CoP. However, on a more positive note, the review made clear that the focus of the

IntelCities e-learning platform should be on the knowledge requirements of citizens and that the technology adopted to deliver this ought to break with the tradition of existing city portals, be more socially inclusive, and offer greater opportunities for communities to participate in their development. With this in mind, the examination went on to benchmark the e-learning systems that existing portals are based on and examined them against the knowledge-transfer and capacity-building requirements they set.

The E-Learning Platform

Table 3 illustrates the results of this benchmarking exercise, presenting the average percentage scores of tools provided by 67 commercial e-learning platforms and compares them against the industry standard (Web CT) & European Dynamics' OSS eOWL system. This benchmarking exercise has in turn produced an OSS (Open Source Standards) approach to e-learning, where the exercise is driven by a small "e" and a capital "L." This has opened up the opportunity to get beyond the tendency for city learning portals to merely provide links to resources held elsewhere and provided the means to customize an e-Learning platform capable of meeting the particular knowledge-transfer requirements of the IntelCities CoP.

The Learning Management System

The Learning Management System (LMS) developed for such purposes lies at the center of the platform. The system provides the common ground between course tutors, trainers, and learners, a virtual space where they can cooperate with one another by sharing experiences and offering personal and confidential advice on available courses, content, and communication tools. It is designed as a set of modules for which tutors can create content, administer the resulting course, and create assessments for learners, while learners are able to work with the related material. The services offered by the LMS are underpinned by a set of repositories holding information on personal data of registered members, learner profiles, material available to support the structured course of studies, and other unstructured data also available to learners.

Table 3: Results of the e-learning Platform Benchmarking Exercise

Learner Tools	Commercial Platforms[1]	WebCT[2]	IntelCities Platform[2]
Communication Tools	57%	71%	86%
Learning Tools	62%	60%	60%
Learner Involvement Tools	64%	75%	100%
Administration Tools	79%	75%	100%
Course Delivery Tools	72%	80%	100%
Course Design	56%	83%	83%
Hardware/Software	70%	80%	63%
Pricing/Licensing	80%	40%	100%

Source: Deakin et al. (2004)
Notes: [1] Indicates average percentage of learner tools covered by the 67 commercial e-learning platforms surveyed. This survey includes those used by Edinburgh, Dublin, Glasgow (Drumchapel), Helsinki (Arabianranta and Munala) and Reykjavic (Garoabaer) and approximately 60 others.
[2] Highlights the percentage of functionality of individual learning tools covered by services available on WebCT and European Dynamics' OSS (e-OWL) platform.

The system architecture rests on three levels, each supported by a dedicated administrator. Here the administrator is responsible for managing the directory of members registered to a course (this provides the interface between the course provider and the learner), while the tutor/trainer will be the course content creator, and the coordinator is responsible for distributing the course(s) to the learners and coordinating the services supporting the related studies. This is supported by core services that provide the learning content, communication, collaboration, assessment, and administration of IntelCities courses (i.e., the learning materials, skills packages, and training exercises used for developing socially-inclusive and participatory urban regeneration programs) that are available to the CoP. (See Figure 2.)

The E-Learning Materials and Courses

The e-learning materials are made up of three IntelCities courses. The first short course is aimed at members of the public with an interest in becoming more

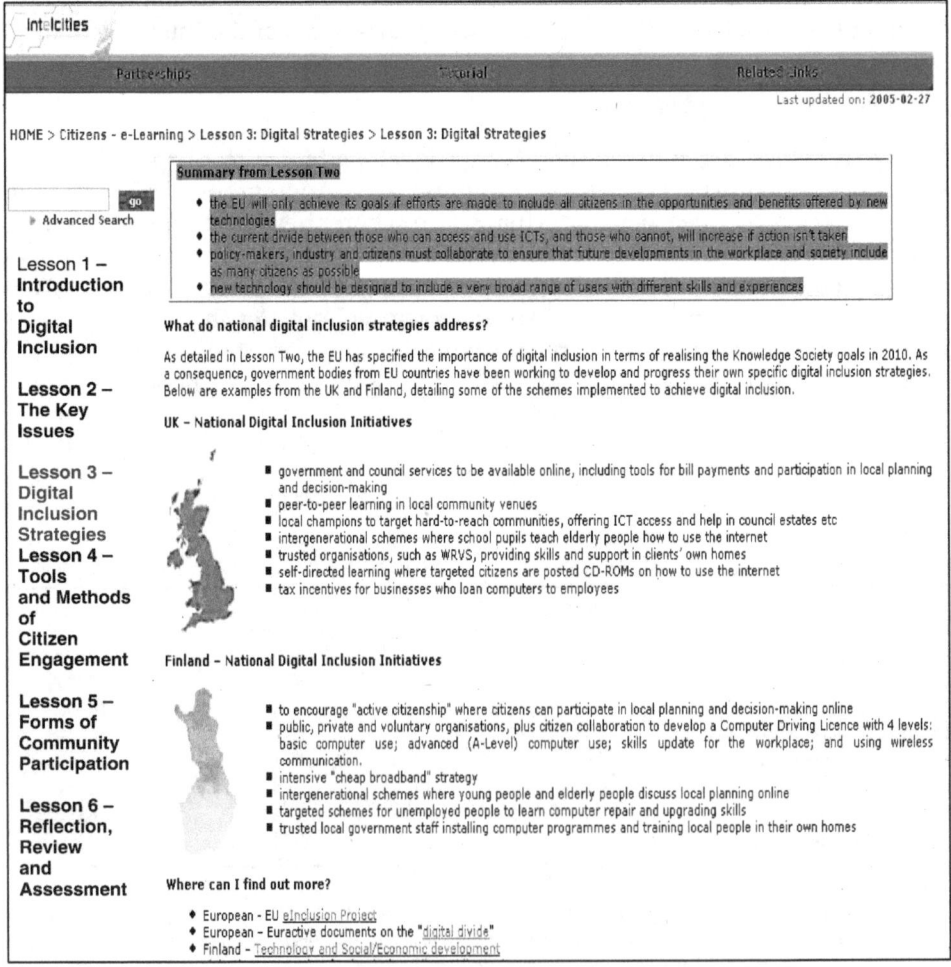

Figure 2. Sample of learning material for the Level 1 (lesson 3) eCitizenship course
Source: <http://elrn.eurodyn.com/edos/elearning/welcome.do>

involved in civic life via the use of new technologies. The second course targets administrators within the public sector: those responsible for meeting citizens' expectations, in terms of access to electronically-enhanced eGov services. The third is aimed at policy-makers and strategists within city administrations who want to make their cities leading examples of the digitally inclusive knowledge society. Together, these three courses make up the CoPs eCitizenship module. Under this heading, the course materials tackle the same core concepts: digital inclusion; citizens' expectations; and the means by which cities can meet the needs of their e-ready citizens, while enabling access for those currently excluded from the knowledge management systems and digital technologies underlying the public's use of online services. The pitch and tone vary accordingly across the suite of materials, yet each progresses the learner towards an understanding of the tools and methods currently available for cities to use to engage citizens as members of an online community.

While the short course on digital inclusion provides a set of "taster" sessions on citizens' engagement with digital technologies, no prior experience of ICTs is needed as a prerequisite for the learning. It is designed to be open to everyone and provide universal access as a bottom line for the learning experiences to follow. Level 2 is targeted at citizens with different levels of experiential learning and, therefore, abilities. Those collaborating on the development of learning materials for Level 2 have developed three representative e-service users, each with different levels of familiarity with ICTs. The novice user is characterized as a citizen with little experience in using computers or the Internet, but an interest in learning how to find information and pay bills online. The semi-skilled, or intermediate-level user is a citizen with regular access to a computer and average-to-good ICT skills. At this level of ICT ability, the citizen is interested in locating detailed, up-to-date information online and in submitting comments and feedback to the city. The advanced user has frequent access to ICTs and is highly skilled and confident in his ability to interact using the Internet. This user wants maximum benefit from new technologies and is keen to interact with the city via services such as online debates and e-petitions.

These three characterizations serve to elicit the relationship between citizens' ICT skills and competencies and the e-services they expect their cities to provide. Figure 3 summarizes this relationship. The left-hand column details the expectations of novice ICT users, the challenges these represent and action cities can take in response to them. With little access to ICTs, such as home PCs or 3G mobile phones, the novice ICT user has little confidence in the e-services under development and the potential benefits they offer. In terms of their priorities, citizens at this level want to know if they can locate new online services easily. The challenge cities face is to meet these very basic requirements without alienating those with higher skill levels.

As Figure 3 indicates, citizens with minimal ICT skills are unable to make use of cutting-edge, interactive technologies. Digitally excluded citizens, often among the most socially deprived, risk being further marginalized because they lack the skills to progress in the workplace and are not members of the online communities where citizens and their cities consult with one another and meet to deliberate on issues of public concern. By investing in community-based training initiatives and online user support, cities ensure that citizens with little-or-no-ICT experience are offered the chance to develop their skills, to be included, and to participate in the customization and co-design of more complex inter-active online activities.

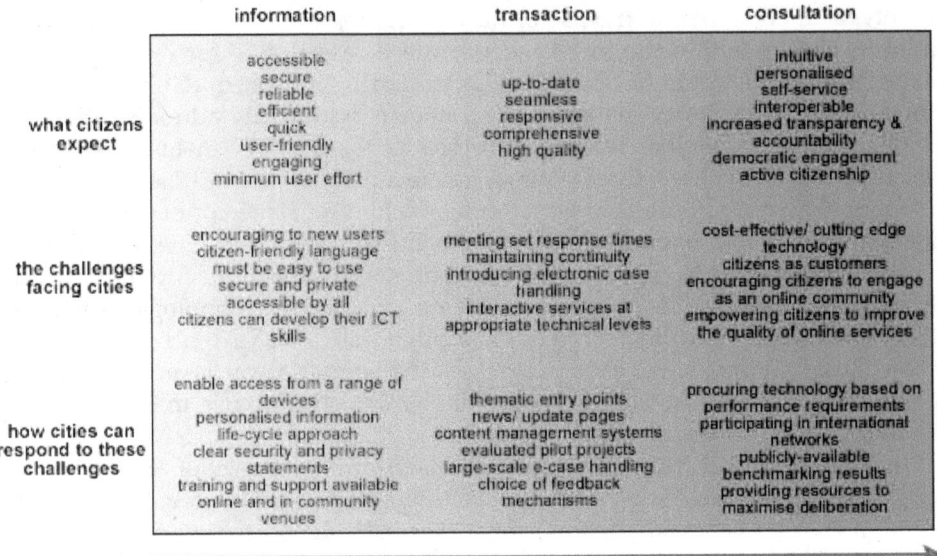

Figure 3. Citizens' skills and competencies
Source: Campbell and Deakin (2005)

Figure 3 identifies citizens at the lowest skill level as seeking engagement at an informational level. Citizens who have progressed beyond basic ICT skills are referred to as those seeking engagement at a transactional level. The semi-skilled, or intermediate level, user has better access to ICTs than the novice and is already comfortable accessing basic information and making bill payments online. It also identifies the intermediate user's expectations: for up to-date information of a high quality and the seamless transition between different online services and websites.

As with the novice user, the user at this level requires services that are pitched at the appropriate skill level, again presenting the city with the challenge of meeting the needs of a diverse society. At this "transactional" level, citizens are interested in establishing online communication with the city, and in order to engage these users and encourage repeated use of such services, cities are required to respond within set times. Electronic case handling is listed in Figure 3 as one method of managing the information flow and building citizens' trust in e-services, as are content management systems to ensure continuity across a range of web pages and services.

Citizens with advanced ICT skills and regular access pose an additional set of challenges to their cities, given their expectations of personalized and intuitive services like those offered in e-commerce. However, citizens at this level of ability are also able to make use of the more complex technologies cities can offer to encourage online consultative and deliberative participation. By engaging increasing numbers of citizens in online dialogue, city administrations harness the knowledge and experiences of local people in order to improve the quality of services they customize by way of and through their co-design.

The Level 3 set of lessons examines the skill bases and competencies of users who have just such abilities, who expect their city to provide personalized and intuitive services, and to make use of the more complex technologies cities can offer to encourage online consultation and deliberative participation. Level 3 provides a set of lessons on how cities can use the skills and competencies their citizens have to make use of these complex technologies and become leading examples of the IntelCities CoP. Two inter-active video lessons have also been produced to support this set of lessons.

The Pedagogy

The pedagogy of the course materials is grounded in the transformational logic of situational learning, very much action-orientated and problem-based in the sense that the platform's knowledge-transfer capacity is framed in "structured query language" (SQL) protocols. This can be classified as follows:

- for the basic level of learning, it is instructional, providing an outline of the materials to be mastered
- for the intermediate level user, the pedagogy is again instructional, but the emphasis here is on the social context of the eCity platform and sets out the skill bases, competencies, and training needed for citizens to use the services and engage with others by carrying out online transactions, or by consulting with others as members of a community
- the pedagogy of the advanced learner is constructivist. Drawing upon the learning of the previous level, this course uses this knowledge as a platform for citizens to use as a means of intervening in decision-making processes, engaging in consultations, and deliberating with others to influence the level of government service provision. Here, users of the eCity platform learn how to actively participate as members of an online community that seeks to democratize decision-making and develop the degree of reciprocity that is needed to build trust between citizens and the organizations governing the delivery of services.

Having established the user requirements and found an e-Learning platform to carry them, attention has turned to developing this as a knowledge-management system and digital library supporting the activities of the IntelCities CoP. Developed as back-office functions, attention has subsequently been given to integrating the system and library into the IntelCities middleware and delivering information about the pool of eGov services to citizens wanting to learn about them.

The Knowledge-Management System and Digital Library

The knowledge-management system is organized and grouped according to the requirements of a pre-specified, but evolving, eGov services ontology. The overriding objective of the IntelCities CoP is to provide an e-learning platform that allows access to a knowledge-management system and that is both accessible and useable. This objective has been met by developing the knowledge-management system's Document Manager (DM). The DM that has been developed has the capacity to perform ontology-based annotation in Semantic Web for the easy creation, application, and use of semantic data. (The Semantic Web allows users to share content beyond the boundaries of applications and websites.) This is particularly important where learners require the KMS to perform a deep and semantically-rich annotation of materials.

The digital library is the electronic repository storing the information available for extraction by the knowledge-management system. The rationale for developing the digital library as part of the knowledge-management system lies with the potential the DM has to function as a service capable of:

- capturing, storing, indexing, and (re)distributing the learning materials, skill packages, and training manuals
- extending this to include the formal semantics (metadata, knowledge) for the retrieval and extraction of the said materials, packages, and manuals available to support the integrated modeling of eGov services
- offering access to the extensive range of products stored as knowledge objects in the digital library and available for extraction by those managing the development of the middleware as a platform for pooling eGov services together and extending delivery of them to citizens as front-end users.

Semantically Interoperable E-Government Services

Using the Semantic Web paradigm, the e-learning platform is capable of delivering data to its users in a way that enables a more effective "query-minded" discovery, integration, and reuse of the knowledge that can be accessed from the digital library. Through the platform's utilization of Semantic Web technologies, data uploaded by the knowledge-management system (as information available from the system's DM) presents knowledge products codified in ways that not only correspond to documents (web pages, images, audio clips, etc. as the Internet currently does), but more pre-defined objects, such as people, places, organizations, and events that are deposited in the digital library. Using a pre-defined ontology of this type, the DM allows multiple relations among objects to be created.

It is here the IntelCities project achieves its goal of integrating the two types of CoPs and builds the capacity for the organization to be both innovation-seeking and knowledge-generating in the sense that the organization is able to co-design eGov services as semantically-interoperable codifications of the objects they relate to. Currently none of the e-learning platforms forming the basis of the CoP's S.W.O.T. analysis offers such services. Until now it has only been common to see references to the possible convergence of e-learning platforms, knowledge-management systems, and digital libraries. This platform and system get beyond the call for the convergence of such technologies and begins to integrate eGov services with the ICTs available to achieve it. Perhaps most importantly of all, the outcome of all this is an e-learning platform, knowledge-management system, and digital library with the embedded intelligence cities need to deliver semantically interoperable eGov services and meet this requirement as a standard measure of the socially-inclusive and participatory urban regeneration programs the IntelCities CoP has a particular interest in.

Integration into the eCity Platform

Figure 4 illustrates how the IntelCities CoP proposes integrating the e-learning platform, the knowledge-management system, and the digital library and shows the workflow supporting this. The figure shows the workflow as having

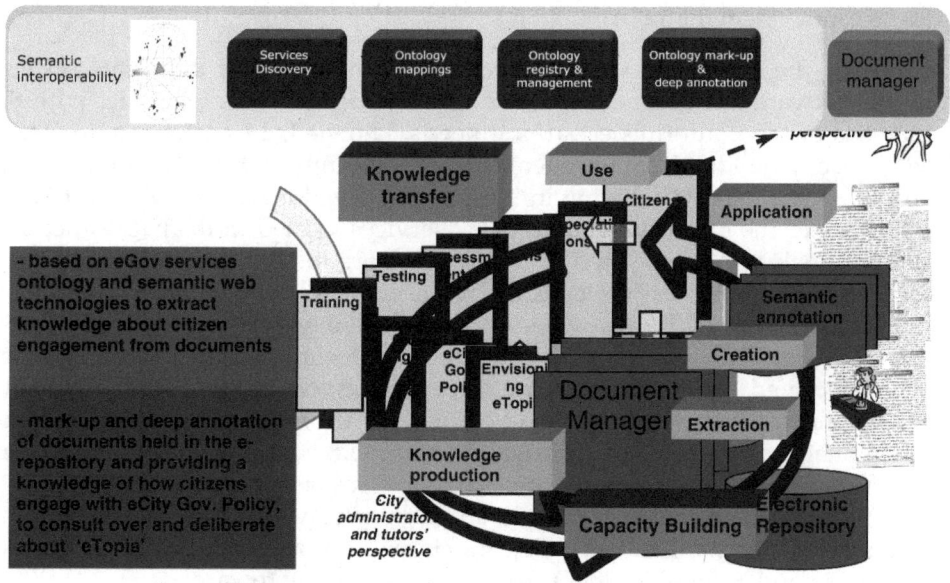

Figure 4. Integration into the eCity platform

its basis in the digital library and the knowledge-management system of the e-Learning platform. It also shows the workflow between the courses held on the platform and the knowledge-management system. Here the system's DM is shown to semantically annotate the learning materials, skill packages, and training manuals supporting the courses held on the platform and mark them up in line with the index and classification of the eGov services ontology evolving to manage the knowledge drawn from the digital library.

These back-office functions, in turn, lead to the creation of the citizen engagement matrix, designed as a semantically-rich grid, allowing communities to be inclusive and actively participate (via consultative and deliberative operations) in the development of the middleware as applications that this platform of eGov services delivers to the front-end. These developments provide the knowledge management toolkit. This term is preferred to "e-learning platform" because this best captures the contribution the tools (the electronic repository, the document manager, the semantic annotation, and the mark-up system) make to the type of knowledge management and digital library services currently found on city portals.

While it is recognized that this journey—from front-end, e-government services to the middleware and back-office functions—represents a significant detour, it is undertaken because the path taken does mark a significant step forward, not only in terms of the additional learning services that existing city portals are now able to offer, but in "squaring of the circle" and providing a platform with the intelligence—the knowledge-management system and the digital library—to integrate the front, middle, and back-office sections of their organization as a virtual CoP. This CoP is based on standards that are interoperable across a growing pool of extensible eGov services and have the capacity, customization qualities, and co-design features to support socially-inclusive and participatory urban regeneration programs.

The "eTopia" Demonstrator

At present, the integration we have been describing is mainly technical, concerning the software developments needed to host such services and meet with the semantics of the platform's e-learning needs, knowledge-transfer requirements, and capacity-building commitments. This currently takes the form of an "eTopia" demonstrator, showing in "session-managed logic" how the eCity platform accesses the extensive pool of eGov services located in the back-office and uses the intelligence embedded in the middleware to deliver Level 3 (advanced e-Citizenship) courses on the consultative needs and deliberative requirements of such developments. This provides a "real time demonstration" of the platform's capacity to be "SMART" in developing both the technical and semantically-rich content required for the middleware to begin supporting the socially-inclusive consultations and participatory deliberations of urban regeneration programs. These enhanced processes of consultation and deliberation also have the advantage of offering citizens multi-channel access to eGov services that are customized, co-designed, and bundled together as socially inclusive and participatory urban regeneration, programmed for bringing about improvements in the quality of life (Deakin and Allwinkle, 2007). This goes a long way toward:

- uncovering the business logic upon which to base the intelligence-driven (re)organization of cities and the standards that can be used as benchmarks against which to measure the performance of the platform
- revealing the performance-based measures needed to assess whether any plans cities possess to develop eGov services (over the platform) have the embedded intelligence (the learning, knowledge-based competencies, and skills) required to support such actions
- providing the means to evaluate whether planned developments build the (intellectual) capacity—learning, knowledge-based competencies, and skills—needed to support such actions.

Testing the Demonstrator

In addition to developing the semantically-interoperable eGov services, the IntelCities' CoP has also sought to evaluate how well they perform as components of the eCity platform. This has meant developing three "eTopia demonstrator" storylines, where a group of typical learners, such as those referred to previously, use the eCity platform to query the development of urban regeneration programs by either searching for information on a given initiative, gaining access to possible online transactions supporting any such actions, or getting involved in the customization and co-design of those consultations and deliberations underlying the governance of such proposals.

The three storylines develop scenarios for:

- accessing local services in neighborhoods subject to regeneration
- carrying out online transactions related to the use of land
- consulting and deliberating on safety and security issues underlying the governance of urban regeneration programs.

The storylines aim to fulfill three requirements: first, to continue the loosely structured scenarios used to demonstrate the significance of the citizen-led learning agenda developed under the alpha version of the eCity platform; second, to integrate this into the back-office business logic of the beta version testing of the eCity platform; and third, to establish whether the interoperability resulting from the vertical and horizontal integration of the services is beneficial because it enables urban regeneration programs to work better in meeting citizens' expectations. The following summarizes the scenario-based testing of the third and "advanced" level of eCitizenship held on the e-learning platform and accessed via the knowledge-management system.

The exercise involved an "integrated eGov services scenario" in which two people, Mark and Sarah, are keen to discover what governance services the eCity platform offers and how it is possible to become actively involved in initiatives promoted to tackle problems associated with crime in their neighborhood. The material demonstrates the ways in which Mark and Sarah can use the eCity platform (vis-à-vis, the e-learning platform and knowledge-management system) to not only learn about what they can do to tackle crime, but to gain knowledge of how the community's participation in such initiatives can lead to the development of safe and secure neighborhoods.

The Integrated eGov Services Scenario

Both Mark and Sarah feel their family and work commitments have prevented them from becoming more involved with local groups in the past. However, both are keen on home computing and have broadband connections to the Internet. Mark feels that the city's website should provide information on crime rates and proposes that he and Sarah should log-on and initiate a search to see how much they can learn about crime prevention initiatives online. They both want to know what their local administration is currently doing to address neighborhood issues across the city and to submit their comments on past and present initiatives. They also feel it would be valuable to see what local groups are doing to tackle crime and whether any operate in their neighborhood. They are also keen to discover how they, as citizens, can use the platform of services available on the city's information portal to ensure that the urban regeneration programs affecting their neighborhood are effective in tackling crime and making the areas safe and secure. Mark's work frequently takes him to one of the country's larger cities, and he has been impressed by the local initiatives in other cities that address neighborhood issues. He is also interested in comparing the crime rates in his neighborhood with those in other cities and finding which crime-prevention schemes seem to work best.

The Steps

The steps Mark and Sarah can take to use the eCity platform in begin tackling the problems they encounter are set out in Table 4.

The Information Flow

The flowchart in Figure 5 demonstrates how the eCity platform helps Mark and Sarah query the developments they have a particular interest in and use this to find the information they need. They are able to access a wide range of data sets from their local administration, such as policy documents and strategies but, most importantly, they are able to exploit the potential to use this information to interact with other like-minded people as part of a larger group. In this aim, Mark and Sarah can develop a web page and host it on the city's learning plat-

Table 4: Step-wise logic of the service discovery

Step 1	Using the city's website, view information on current neighborhood policies, strategies, and targets
Step 2	Use the website to access a list of current public consultants
Step 3	Use the search tools to learn about any local online crime prevention and environmental clean-up groups, run either by local people or by the city
Step 4	Use the neighborhood reporting service on the interactive maps to report problems such as abandoned cars, graffiti, and fly tipping
Step 5	Set up a web page for local people interested in tackling crime, security, and environmental programs
Step 6	Post comments on the city's discussion boards
Step 7	See how the city compares to other cities on issues like crime and pollution
Step 8	Submit a formal e-petition, setting out an agenda for tackling these types of neighborhood issues.

form, setting out their concerns about crime and encouraging others to join them as members of an online community discussing how the city should tackle neighborhood safety and security issues. As an online community, they are also able to compare their city's agenda for tackling crime with those of other administrations and learn about good practice examples from elsewhere. These materials can, in turn, be used to shape the community's online discussions and enable Mark and Sarah to submit a formal e-petition to those responsible for leading the development of such initiatives. The "one-stop shop" approach of the eCity platform offers them a range of benefits, such as:

- accessing information from a wide range of city departments and databases at any time of day or night, from any location
- locating relevant information in an interesting, quick, hassle-free way
- employing user-friendly search facilities that offer clearly signposted routes to relevant information
- being able to personalize a web site hosted by the city in order to engage other local groups or individuals
- being able to add useful features to personalized spaces such as mailing list sign-ups and links to other pages
- providing a range of starting points and options to either continue or end the search at various points
- allowing users to consider how the information they obtain affects them, easily contribute their comments/feedback, and actively promote change.

Meeting Citizens' Expectations

The results of this testing exercise are encouraging. Table 5 demonstrates the responses of the group who participated in the test. As this shows, all found the scenarios, steps, and information flow to be understandable in terms of the vocabulary used and also easy to follow. One respondent commented, "I found the material quite open, easy to understand. It made me think more about how I would go about things in the future." As Table 5 also illustrates, most of those participating in the testing exercise found the demonstration to offer a useful representation of how to learn about the eCity platform's online services and use the information uploads to transfer knowledge about their communities.

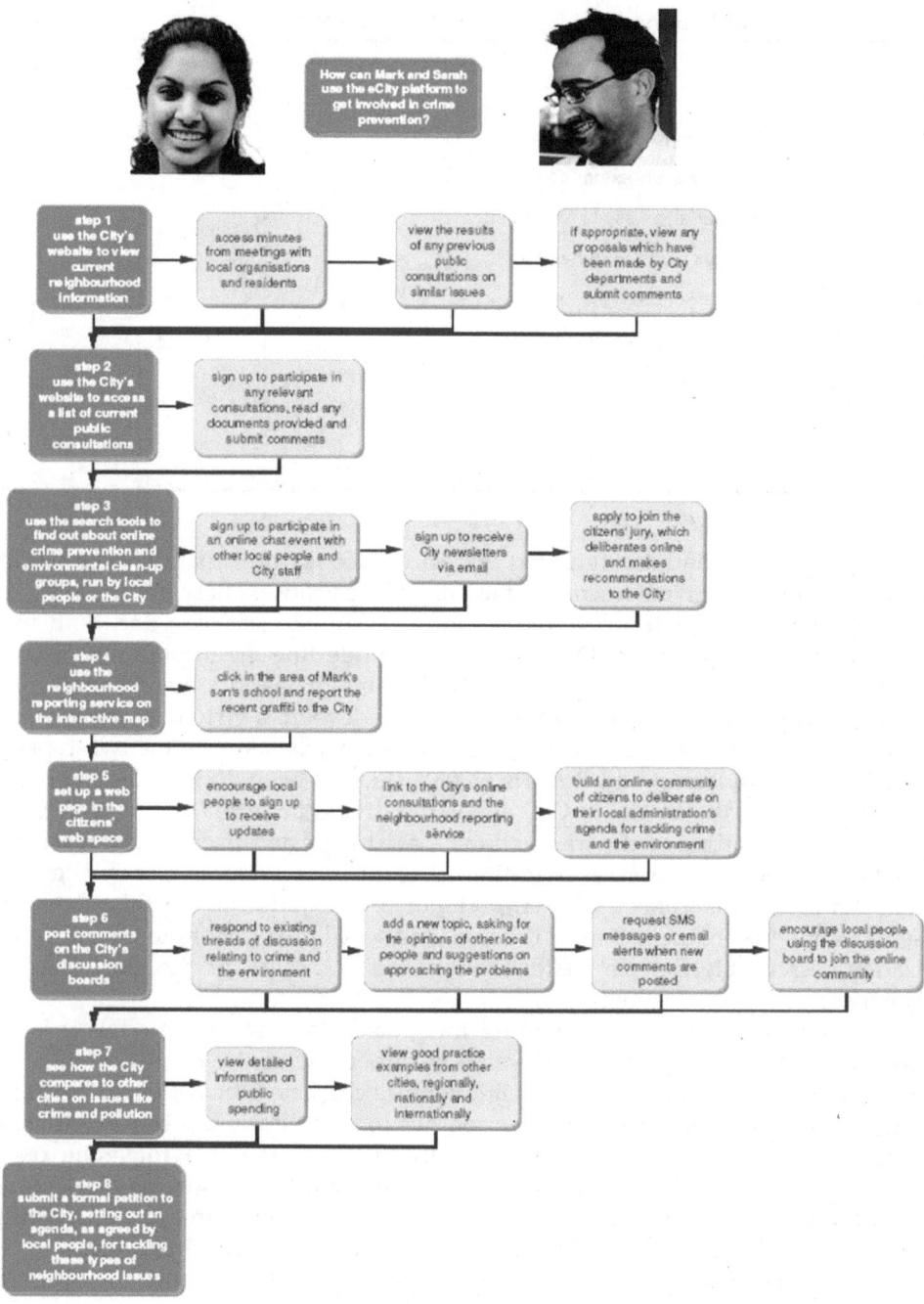

Figure 5. Information flow of the testing scenario

Conclusion

This paper has argued that IntelCities CoP is innovation-seeking because the network provides an example of a virtual organization whose customization is co-designed to manage the learning needs and knowledge-generating requirements of a technological platform.

Table 5: Feedback responses to the scenario

feedback responses (as %) - Manchester 2	yes	not sure	no
Was the tone of the material appropriate?	72	28	
Was the vocabulary understandable?	100		
Was the text clear and easy to follow?	100		
Was the example of Mark and Sarah helpful?	72		28
Was the material about the right length?	86	14	
Did the diagrams help your understanding of the material?	72	14	14

Key: yes   not sure   no

The examination has suggested there are three features that define the IntelCities CoP and that give it a sense of meaning and purpose. These are: building the capacity for shared enterprise, the co-design of online services, and both their monitoring and evaluation. It has gone on to underline the importance of these as characteristics of the IntelCities CoP and in this aim has added another six qualities that have been exploited by the network to develop a virtual learning organization that is capable of bridging the gap which exists between the two types of CoPs outlined by Amin and Roberts (2008). This has been done in the interest of illustrating how the IntelCity CoP spans the divide between what are in crude terms representatives of the transactional-based logic and user-centric reasoning of eGov service provision. The additional features referred to clearly highlight these qualities and reflect their importance, but in addition to this, they also serve to underscore the technical rational, and social purpose of the virtual organization responsible for the customization and co-design of the electronically-enhanced service provision.

This suggests that in developing integrated eGov service models it is not possible for intelligent cities to develop as either one or the other type of CoPs because the shared enterprise and joint venture characteristics of virtual learning organizations means their customization has to be co-designed in ways that are both innovation-seeking and also knowledge-generating. Having gone on to discuss the technical solutions adopted to integrate the eGov services model with the legacy systems operated by cities involved in this enterprise, attention turned to the SOA adopted as the business model for the eCity platform.

As has been shown, these developments are valuable because they provide the means to address the criticisms of the learning services currently available on city portals and offer the opportunity for the emerging technologies of the e-learning platform, knowledge-management systems, and digital libraries to meet the learning needs, knowledge-transfer requirements, and capacity-building commitments of the IntelCities CoP. This it has been suggested, marks a significant step forward in the development of learning services and offers the opportunity for platforms of this type to develop as knowledge-management systems supported by digital libraries. In view of this, we have suggested that if the full significance of these technical innovations is to be realized, then this integration needs to progress and requires systems developed for these purposes to not only be interoperable across the IntelCities middleware, but all the eGov services which are available to citizens at the front-end. The way in which the IntelCities CoP proposes to achieve this is particularly innovative because the organization offers a strategy to consolidate the underlying learning aspirations of city portals, but as particular types of eGov services that have previously remained beyond the reach of the platforms developed for these purposes.

Notes

1. "Communities of practice are groups of people who share a concern or a passion for something they do and learn how to do it better as they interact regularly" <www.ewenger.com/theory/>
2. While the title of the article by Amin and Roberts (2008) goes under the name of "Beyond Communities of Practice," they use the phrase to suggest the need to "get beyond" the "undifferentiated" use of the term and the requirement for more "contextualized" studies of the type set out in this paper.

Bibliography

A. Amin and J. Roberts, "Knowing in Action: Beyond Communities of Practice," *Research Policy* 37 (2008) 353–369.

C. Berger, K. Möslein, F. Piller, and R. Reichwald, "Cooperation Between Manufacturers, Retailers, and Customers for User Co-Design: Learning from Exploratory Research," *European Management Review* 1 (2005) 70–87.

T. Binder, E. Brandt, and J. Gregory, "Design Participation(s): A Creative Commons for Ongoing Change," *CoDesign* 4:2 (2008) 79–83.

F. Campbell and M. Deakin, "Cities as Leading Examples of Digitally-Inclusive Knowledge Societies: The E-Citizenship Course, Representative Users, Pedagogy, and Engagement Matrix," in M. Osborne and B. Wilson, eds., *Making Knowledge Work* (Stirling: Stirling University, 2005).

S. Curwell, M. Deakin, I. Cooper, K. Paskaleva-Shapira, J. Ravetz, and D. Babicki, "Citizens' Expectations of Information Cities: Implications for Urban Planning and Design," *Building Research and Information* 22:1 (2005) 55–66.

M. Deakin, "e-Topia, SUD, and ICTs: Taking the Digitally-Inclusive Urban Regeneration Thesis Full Circle," *Journal of Urban Technology* 14:3 (2007) 131–139.

M. Deakin and S. Allwinkle, "e-Topia, SUD, and ICTs: The Post-Human Nature, Embedded Intelligence, Cyborg-Self, and Agency of Digitally-Inclusive Regeneration Platforms," *International Journal of the Humanities* 5:2 (2007) 199–208.

M. Deakin and S. Allwinkle, "Urban Regeneration and Sustainable Communities: The Role of Networks, Innovation and Creativity in Building Successful Partnerships," *Journal of Urban Technology* 14:1 (2007) 77–91.

M. Deakin and S. Allwinkle, "The IntelCities Community of Practice: The E-Learning Platform, Knowledge Management System, and Digital Library for Semantically-Interoperable e-Governance Services," *International Journal of Knowledge, Culture and Change Management* 6:3 (2006) 155–162.

M. Deakin, K. Van Isacker, and A. Wong, *Review of the IntelCities Knowledge Capture Requirements Using a S.W.O.T. Analysis* (Edinburgh: Edinburgh, Napier University, 2004).

D. Ellis, R. Oldridge, and A. Vasconcelos, "Community and Virtual Community," *Annual Review of Information Sciences and Technology* 38 (2004) 146–186.

S. Graham and S. Marvin, *Telecommunications and the City* (London: Routledge, 1996).

C. Johnson, "A Survey of Current Research on Online Communities of Practice," *Internet and Higher Education* 4 (2001) 45–60.

U. Josefsson, "Coping with Illness Online: The Case of Patients' Online Communities," *The Information Society* 21 (2005) 143–153.

P. Lombardi, I. Cooper, K. Paskaleva, and M. Deakin, "The Challenge of Designing User-Centric E-Services: Europe Dimensions," in C. Riddeck, ed., *Research Strategies for E-Government Service Adoption* (Hershey: Idea Group Publishing, 2009).

P. Lombardi and S. Curwell, "INTELCITY Scenarios for the City of the Future," in D. Miller and D. Patassini, eds., *Beyond Benefit Cost Analysis* (Aldershot: Ashgate, 2005).

W. Mitchell, *e-Topia: Urban Life, Jim But Not as You Know It* (Cambridge, Massachusetts: MIT Press, 2000).

F. Nikolaus, P. Keinz, and M. Schreier, "Complementing Mass Customization Toolkits with User Communities: How Peer Input Improves Customer Self-Design," *Journal of Product Innovation Management* 256 (2008) 546–559.

C. Osterlund, *Learning across Contexts* (Aarhus: Aarhus University, 1996).

J. Orr, *Talking about Machines: An Ethnography of a Modern Job* (New York: IRL Press, an imprint of Cornell University Press, 1996).

E. Wenger, *Communities of Practice: Learning, Meaning, and Identity* (Cambridge: Cambridge University Press, 1998).

E. Wenger, "Communities of Practice and Social Learning Systems," *Organization* 7:2 (2000) 225–246.

The Business Models and Information Architectures of Smart Cities

George Kuk and Marijn Janssen

ABSTRACT *In the Netherlands, there are two ways cities acquire the smart city status: one way has business models preceding information architecture and the other takes an opposite direction. We used two cities to examine the underlying differences of these two approaches in terms of service enhancement, resource implications, and the sustainability of service development. The first case focused on creating business value through the use of technology by enhancing existing services and/or bringing new services whereas the second case started with creating an infrastructure that served as a technology platform to induce changes in business practices. We found that the first case accumulated business value faster with more new services made available to the public. In contrast, the second case was more resource-intensive and relatively slower in bringing new services to the general public, yet the services were much improved and sustainable over time.*

Introduction

National and local governments have increasingly exploited new and smart technologies to change the ways they interact with their citizens, in that, technologies are used to provide novel and interactive services. Yet the changes underpinning the creation of a smart city come with a series of challenges including: how to determine which new services to develop and which business models to adopt (e.g., can a citizen-centric approach provide a robust model in the development of new services?); how do new services and/or business models change the established ones and affect the existing information architecture (e.g., can we develop new services without being constrained by the existing information architecture?); and notably can the sustainability of changes be assessed (e.g., can we keep on introducing new services?).

Smart cities require an innovative set of services that provide information (and transaction possibilities) to all citizens and businesses about all aspects of city life via interactive, city-wide, Internet-based applications. Cities are becoming aware that, to introduce smart cities, they require new business models for the delivery of services to their constituents. Citizens and businesses have new expectations of what their municipalities have to offer them and expect: the integration of various products into a single service, the reuse and real-time availability of information, easy interaction, and discussion with government bodies. These expectations influence the business models. A business model is derived from the main mission and strategy of a public organization and contains the rationale and elements required to fulfill the mission successfully and captures that rationale to generate value (Janssen et al., 2008; Keen and Qureshi, 2006). The rationale includes the relationship between an agency's strategy and information architecture (architecture for short in this paper), which both limits and enables business models. As a result, the realization of smart cities and the accompanying business rationales require working in tandem with the underlying information architecture.

This raises the question as to how local governments can meet their customers' expectations by transforming their business models and information architectures. Sharma and Gupta (2003) state that planning the transformation towards e-government is the single most important issue facing governments today. Many authors who have identified various growth stages (Andersen and Henriksen, 2006; Klievink and Janssen. 2009; Layne and Lee, 2001). Layne and Lee (2001) focus mainly on the municipal level and identify four growth stages: cataloguing, transaction, vertical integration, and horizontal integration. Although they explain these stages in terms of the various levels of integration and complexity involved, they do not explore new business models and information architecture.

Many municipalities in the Netherlands are moving towards the smart cities concept by exploring new web-based business models to reform their online business practices. This plays an important role within various social, economic, and political relationships that underpin urban life (Dabinett, 2005). Deliberate or not, many municipalities are moving towards the arrangement of a full-service provider (FSP) business model. A FSP refers to the situation that an organizations tries to provide a full range of services directly and via allies owning the customer relationship (Weill and Vitale, 2001). This model facilitates customer interaction through direct information and service provisioning, and involves the collaboration among a number of departments including previously disjointed organizations to provide all services in a one-stop shop (e.g., Janssen et al., 2008; Weill and Vitale, 2001). Despite its intuitive appeal, the FSP model might not suit all types of public agencies and is likely to comprise different steps and enterprise-wide technological changes.

The design and realization of such an enterprise-wide project is a massive and complex undertaking (Hazlett and Hill, 2003), and is prone to failure (Scholl, 2006). This is particularly true considering that the activities and resources required to involve and coordinate many agencies, and that each agency is likely to come with its own heterogeneous set of systems that give rise to all sorts of legacy integration problems. Hence, the realization of FSP might take many more steps and resources than anticipated. Individual agencies have to discern which business model suits their business strategies and requirements better by reexamining the underlying logic and reevaluating whether their existing e-government models are achieving the desired customer-orientation (Janssen et al., 2008). The rush mentality of adopting e-government solutions can easily result in copying each others' features in terms of characteristics, functions, and ideas, rather than looking at the customers' needs and then deciding which business model best satisfies their requirements.

The goal of this paper is to shed light on the transformation process involved in adapting new business models, with a particular focus on the relationship between business models and information architecture. For this purpose, we analyze the business models and the information architectures in two different types of case studies and contrast their efforts. The paper is structured as follows: in the next section, overviews of business models and information architecture are presented. Thereafter, two case studies are presented, and then followed by a discussion of the different transformation strategies and information architecture efforts. Finally conclusions are drawn.

Background

Business Models

In the late 1990s, website monitors were introduced to compare government websites. This stimulated agencies to develop their e-government activities by benchmarking their efforts with others, which in turn resulted in a kind of competition among agencies, with many local politicians expressing the ambition of having the best websites. As a result of these developments, many government agencies were in a hurry to jump on the e-government bandwagon (Kuk, 2003). To a considerable extent, website design became about copying features from other websites, with the aim of scoring high on the monitor. Many government agencies, in their rush to realize these ambitions, failed to pay attention to their missions and the underlying business rationale, which is often used as a synonym for the term business model. Competing on the basis of features instead became more important to them than designing a business rationale that matched their organizations' missions, strategies, products, and customer segments. This, in spite of the fact that, in theory, different organizations are expected to adopt different strategies and business models (e.g., Weltevreden et al., 2005).

Recently, the term "business model" was introduced to refer to the underlying business rationale. The term was coined in the dot.com era (Keen and Qureshi, 2006) and refers to the way an organizational strategy and its web-based systems are connected (Hedman and Kalling, 2003). In contrast to e-commerce models, e-government business models use the Internet to add value in areas ranging from service delivery and enforcement to political involvement. This includes a wide range of activities involving interacting with constituents within a given geographical area.

Although e-commerce literature provides a large number of business models (Afuah and Tucci, 2000; Mahadevan, 2000; Rappa, 2002; Timmers, 1998; Weill and Vitale, 2002), a few of them focus on e-government (Janssen et al., 2008). Although in the past the main focus was on developing a comprehensive list of models, Weill and Vitale (2002) offer eight "atomic" business models for classifying e-commerce websites, which were applied to the e-government domain by Janssen, Kuk, and Wagenaar (2008). (See Table 1.) The underlying idea is that new business models can be created by combining these atomic models. Janssen et al. (2008) provide the characteristics of the various models and their typical functions, as well as examples. Cities can assess their web presence by analyzing their current business models and use the list of business models to determine which best match their mission and strategy.

A smart city usually consists of a number of business models, with one of them often being the full-service provider model. Any realistic understanding of what it means to be a smart city needs to specify the type of business models being used and ensure that the information architecture is able to support the desired business models.

Table 1: Taxonomy of e-government business models

E-Government Business Model	Description
1. Content provider	Providing static and dynamic content, including contact information, organization information, product and service information, and news.
2. Direct-to-customer	Directly providing services to customers and/or businesses. Various stages can be determined, including the information, communication, and transaction stage.
3. Value-net-integrators	Collecting, processing, and distributing information from several organizations. This is a networked type of business model that often focuses on a particular customer segment; for instance, entrepreneurs.
4. Full-service provider	Enabling interaction through directly providing information and services. This involves the collaboration of several departments and/or organizations to create a one-stop shop.
5. Infrastructure service provider	Providing infrastructural services to support the creation of an online presence.
6. Market	Matching the supply and demand with regard to information, human resources, services, or goods; for instance, matching volunteers with requests for volunteers.
7. Collaboration	Providing the instruments and tools needed to participate in activities like policy-making projects and decision-making, including visualization and simulation tools that can be used to predict the implications of policies.
8. Virtual communities	Providing a community of recurring customers, including user-generated and shared content and the sharing of content.

Sources: *Janssen et al., 2008; Weill and Vitale, 2002*

Realizing innovation in business models may not be an easy matter, and it may have far-reaching implications. Henderson and Clark (1990:12) draw a distinction between modular innovation and architectural innovation, which is useful to understanding the relationship between a business model and an information architecture. Modular innovation "involves changing a core technology within an overall system but not the relationships among subsystems," whereas architecture innovation "involves a reconfiguration of existing components in a new way often brought about by an improvement in a component technology." Each innovation requires a different type of expertise. Innovating individual systems involves changing the core technological design, which is what happened with the rise of the Internet, web information systems and, more recently, Web 2.0 technology. Architecture innovation involves the relationship between systems that is made possible by integration technology, which is often also web-based, and by innovation in the separate components.

Information Architecture

In the past, most government organizations developed their own information systems in relative isolation, creating separate information systems for every product or service, which resulted in a fragmented landscape of unrelated systems supporting various business processes, using different data formats provided by different software vendors, written in different languages, and deploying different protocols. In today's environment, citizens and businesses expect a higher degree of transparency through access to information that is stored in the many various systems and to information about policy-making. The fragmented landscape mentioned above makes it difficult to share information effectively, because that often requires collecting the information from various systems, connecting the separate elements, and then providing the results.

Information architecture has to do with using information and managing the relationship between individual systems, with the aim of acquiring, processing, and disseminating the information. Organizations can use information architecture as an instrument to outline their desired architecture, aligning the application landscape, business processes, and information sources and flows. Architecture is relevant in particular to organizations using large numbers of applications, with problems like functional overlap, duplication and inconsistent data, heterogeneous format, and data redundancy.

Although it is a relatively new discipline, the seminal work on enterprise architecture was carried out by Zachman (1987) in the late 1980s. There is no generic definition of information architecture and various definitions have been suggested (Ross, 2003). Over time, the term "information architecture" has been replaced by "enterprise architecture," where enterprise refers to the enterprise-wide scope of the architecture. Because the term "architecture" can also refer to the whole-of-government scope, and information needs to be related, we prefer to use the term information architecture. Generically, architecture is the description of a set of elements and the way they are related (Armour et al., 1999). Because their relationships determine the possibility to access, combine, process, and provide information, they influence the potential of information.

Information architecture can be descriptive and prescriptive, presenting a blueprint of relationships within a system and how these relationships will be realized. Usually, architectures provide a global roadmap for the transformation from an existing situation to an envisioned future one. To realize a prescriptive architecture, programs and projects need to be carried out, which in turn may result in change to both the descriptive and the prescriptive architecture. The fact that an existing architecture is affected by programs and projects may lead to new insights that in turn have an impact on the prescriptive architecture. Architecture encompasses the interconnectedness of applications and the degree to which individual applications need to be integrated.

Linthicum (2003) describes various levels of integration, data application, and user-interface-level integration based on the concept of a three-tier architecture. In a three-tier architecture, the complexity is reduced by differentiating the presentation, business logic, and data layers. Each layer can be changed without affecting the others. The basic idea is that integration can be achieved on each tier.

Research Method

Seeking to examine the relationship between business models and information architecture, we used a comparative case study methodology (Yin, 1989). We compared two cities with contrasting approaches and practices towards the use of business models and information architecture. Both aspired to become smart cities by adapting the business model of a full-service provider. The first case undertook a strategy of enhancing services at the front-end, whereas the second case started with a back-end strategy focusing on the technology. Both cases were investigated using interviews and studying reports. In total, five in-depth interviews were conducted and transcribed. The interviews lasted between one and two hours. Our analysis proceeded through four rounds of coding. In the first round, we coded instances of service enhancements and any changes made to the information architecture. In the second round of coding, each author independently identified the underlying rationales and reasoning of the observed changes both in services and technology. In the third round of coding, we wanted to determine how these changes affected the front-end transactions with the public and how the back-end changes inscribed new roles and practices within and across different departmental agencies. In the final round of coding, we sought to relate the underlying logics of changes to the relationship between business models and information architecture. During each round, we iteratively cross checked and referenced the findings with publicly available information about these two cities.

A general problem that information architectures address is the relationship between the front-end and the back-end, which requires decisions with regard to which processes and activities should take place in view of the customer (at the front-end or front office) or out of the customer's view at the back-end (or back office) (Richardson, 1994; Safizadeh et al., 2003). This directly influences the interactions with customers, as many activities in the front office improve responsiveness and may make it necessary to redesign business processes in such a way that responsibilities are allocated to the front office and to redesign information architecture in such a way that the necessary information is available at the front-end. In general, the front-end includes business processes that are used to interact directly with citizens and/or businesses, whereas the back-end comprises all business processes that do not directly involve customer interactions. The need to keep the front-end and back-end separated is based on their different objectives and characteristics. The main objective of the front-end is to ensure demand-driven service delivery, whereas the main objective of the back-end is to achieve efficiency by processing information quickly at low costs.

Background

The first city is a medium-sized municipality, and the second is a relatively larger municipality. Both municipalities have a myriad of applications with overlapping functionalities. In the past, the IT department of each city procured its own applications, which resulted in a highly fragmented ICT architecture, consisting of many legacy systems. More recently, both municipalities used the service-oriented architecture (SOA) and web services technology as their main standard, as suggested by the Dutch National References architecture (http://www.e-overheid.nl/atlas/referentiearchitectuur/referentiearchitectuur.html).

Case: Web 2.0 Technology for Customer Interaction

The first municipality is a medium-sized municipality with 3,000 employees that is well-known for its innovative services. Over the last five years, its website was considered one of the ten best. It employed a number of technical experts and architects to ensure the continuous improvement of the front-end and all customer contacts. The website was developed and maintained in-house. With regard to the back-end technology, the strategy was to procure software rather than in-source the development of the back-office systems. Although software vendors were not quick when it came to the design and rollout of novel services, this front-end strategy allowed the municipality to save money driven by the citizen-centric approach.

Recently, the focus was on the use of Web 2.0 technologies to integrate the information sources in the clients' web browsers, as shown in Figure 1. Although the same information sources were being used, they were accessible using web services or information feeds. Based on a customer request, a mash-up in that customer's web browser invoked the services and information. From an EAI perspective, this was presented as an instance of user interface integration (Linthicum, 2003). A possible consequence of not including the back-end was that the information was stored on various systems, which increased the chance that information was not consistently maintained.

In addition to providing access to their own information, information from other sources including private, third-parties was also made available. Searchable information included theater schedules, road work, and local events. Because the information was linked to geographical areas, specific districts were responsible for maintaining and ensuring that local content about contacts, events, and crime rates were current. This approach resulted in the use of the community business models, which allowed frequent users to contribute and update content, and in some instances, engaged users in local policy-making.

This type of innovation induced incremental and modular use of technology. For example, the front-end web system was gradually replaced by a newer system

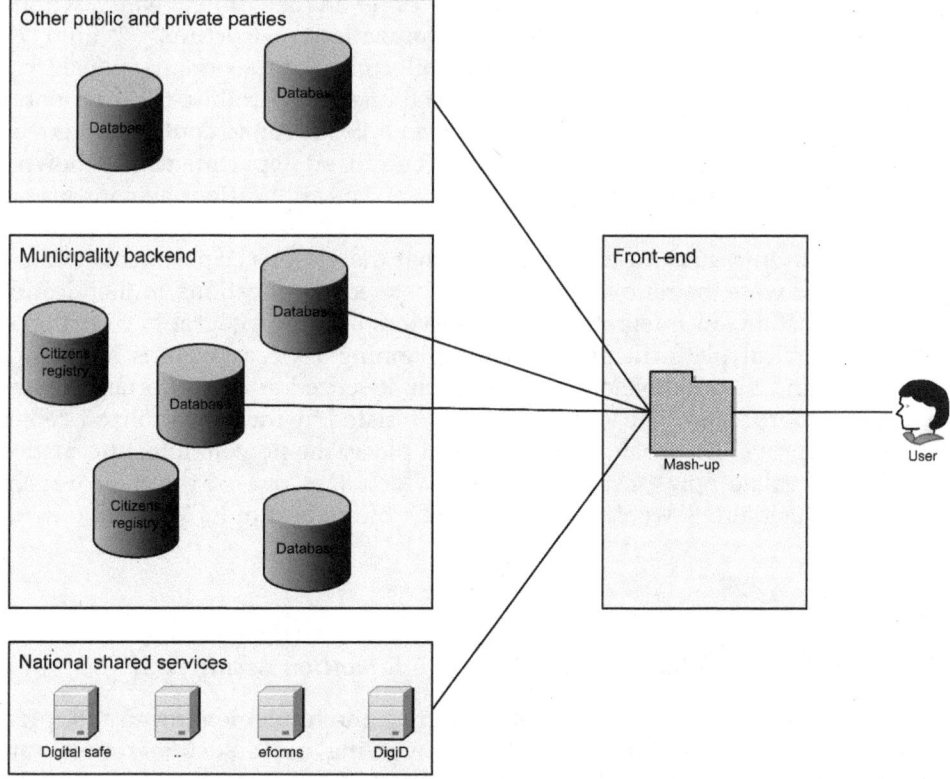

Figure 1. Global overview of architecture

constituted by Web 2.0 technologies. This change had little impact on the rest of the systems. Although this approach resulted in a number of quick wins and the adoption of new business models, it proved difficult to manage in the long run. The numerous links and heterogeneous systems needed to be maintained and this increased control and maintenance costs considerably, taking up most of the IT budget at the expense of further innovation.

Case: Back-End First

The second municipality was one of the largest Dutch municipalities, with 15,000 employees and a large number of departments, in-sourcing all of their applications and business processes. The municipality consisted of 13 city councils and 18 business units, and they were highly autonomous, including making their own decisions on IT procurement. Its website was voted the best website in 2007 and won the "ICT-architecture" award. Its initial approach was primarily about developing a robust infrastructure that allowed the city to integrate and personalize services. An essential element of its strategy was the introduction of a central authentication and identification service (that is linked to the national authentication service), using this system as a basis for creating an infrastructure and platform to integrate many of their systems. Apart from the use of the infrastructure services provided by the national government, the municipality became an infrastructure provider itself and adopted this business model.

One of the interviewees stated that, "A service-oriented architecture enables you to decentralize access to information or to invoke functionality without having to change the decentralized organizational structure." Within the adopted strategy, the match between the architecture and the organizational structure is essential. The main challenge had been one of controlling the information flows and reaching sound service-level agreements (SLAs) to control and govern the exchange of information between the decentralized departments. As shown in Figure 2, this type of integration can be described as application-level integration (Linthicum 2003).

The main infrastructural components that the various departments and city councils used were the rationale for routing between applications, authentication, and identification, an integration of the services and the geographical platform. The geographical platform provided the planning zone as well as a roadmap for current and future development. As such, it served as an important element in terms of coordinating the various projects initiated by the decentralized departments to improve the urban region. Once in place, the new architecture made it possible to realize new business models, which was one of the main reasons that the municipality's website was voted one of the best of its kind nationwide.

Findings and Discussion

Connections between Business Models and Information Architecture

The two case studies demonstrate that designing and implementing an enterprise-wide project is a complex undertaking, involving multiple departments and legacy data, applications, and systems. Although the systems were integrated in both case studies, their approaches were different.

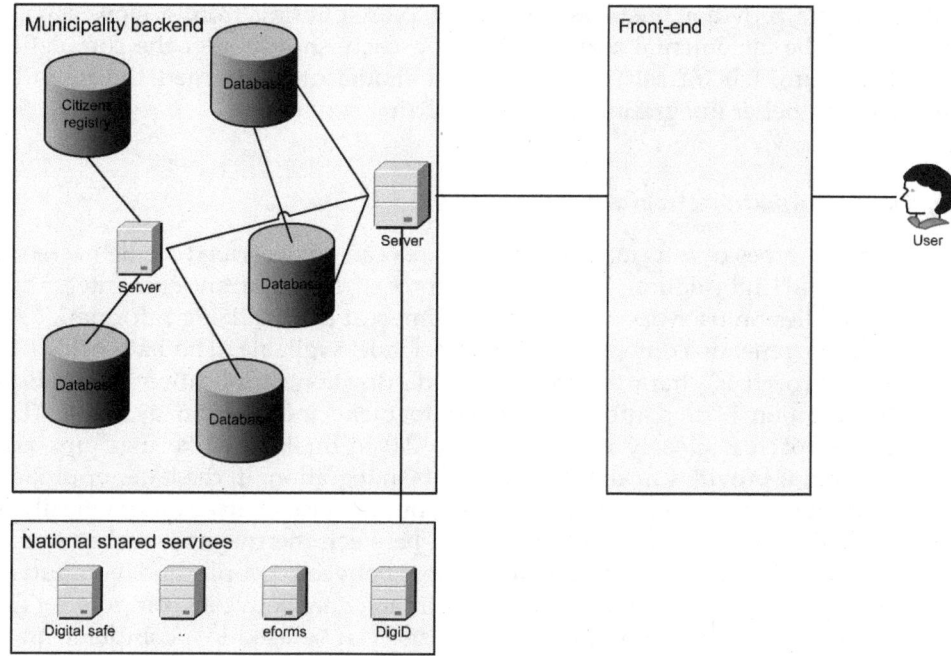

Figure 2. Global overview of architecture

Realizing new business models may be more complex and require more resources than one might expect. Individual agencies have to determine which business models match their particular business strategies and requirements by reexamining the underlying rationale and by deciding whether their existing e-government models are sufficiently customer-oriented (Janssen et al., 2008). The desire to adopt e-government solutions quickly can easily result in copying existing solutions in terms of their characteristics, functions, and ideas, rather than looking at what customers really need and then deciding which business models best meet those needs.

Implementing a business model successfully requires a solid and relevant information architecture that makes it possible to share information stored in individual internal and external systems. Furthermore, new functions have to be developed and implemented. In our case studies, we observed the following changes, which need to be supported by sound information architecture:

- moving back-end functions to the front office to improve responsiveness
- connecting information sources to create integrated service delivery
- sharing functionalities to create shared services
- using external information sources and services
- communicating with customers and using new methods to facilitate customer interaction.

These developments can be viewed as characteristic of transformational government. In both cases, the ambition was to become a full-service provider, although the approaches were different. The first city we studied focused on modular innovation aimed at creating community and collaboration business models. The second was characterized by architectural innovation based on an infrastructure-provider business model. Despite suffering from a slow start in contrast to the incremental and modular approach, shortly after the completion of architecture, the infrastructural-provider model outperformed the modular approach by better integrating and personalizing services

Types of Information Architectures

The primary types of information architectures can be described as the back-end and front-end information integration approaches. The front-end integration approach relies on user-based integration aimed at externalizing information, in which heterogeneous content and data are made available. The back-end integration approach is characterized by standardization, application integration, and the creation of a platform designed to make information available. The former approach is closely related to Web 2.0 technologies like mashups and widgets, and it provides flexibility and ad-hoc integration. In the latter approach, the information cannot only be externalized, but can also be used automatically in business processes. The essential difference between the two approaches is that former approach focuses on the interaction between people and computers, whereas the latter approach is based on interaction between computers. The two approaches are not mutually exclusive and can be used in a complementary way to generate synergetic benefits

Transformation Strategies

The case studies show two opposing transformation strategies, one of which focuses on modular innovation of the front-end, using Web 2.0 technology without considering the back-end systems, for which they rely on software vendors. An important element in the approach of the municipality involved is the ability to provide access to information and to integrate the various information sources on their website. Because transaction volumes are limited, this is a feasible strategy for a medium-sized municipality.

By contrast, the municipality in the second case study decided first to create its technology platforms and infrastructure and then improve its business models. It proved impossible to reengineer the entire organizational structure, which created a need for an infrastructure that was able to provide a platform for the next step, which meant that this municipality adopted the infrastructure-provider business model that involved developing a number of basic infrastructure facilities that make it possible to share (geographical) information and allow various organizational elements to work together.

Figure 3 shows the two transformation strategies. Both municipalities started in the left bottom corner and their ambition was to end up in the top right corner, as full-service providers. In the first case study, the municipality decided to move up first, relying on software vendors to move to the right and realize its ambition. By contrast, in the second case study, the municipality decided to move to the right first and then move upwards.

The former approach is known as modular innovation. One of its main advantages is that it makes it possible to realize quick gains, although in the long run there will be problems with avoiding functional overlap, inconsistent data, and poor information quality as a result of heterogeneous format and data

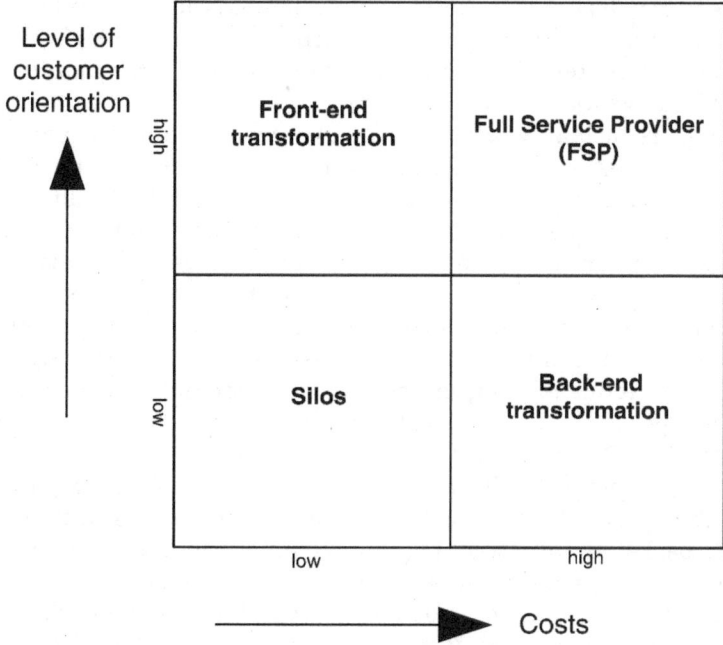

Figure 3. Transformation strategies

redundancy. Furthermore, more and more IT-related resources were needed to maintain the links. The latter approach focuses on architectural innovation, by modifying the back-end. As a result, it will take longer for the benefits to kick in, but once the back-end is ready, it will make becoming a full-service provider an easier move. In the long run, that would appear to make the latter approach a more attractive proposition.

The ideal is to start from the bottom left corner and move directly to the top right corner in Figure 3. Although at face value, this may appear to be the most attractive approach, it may turn out to be trickier than expected, due to a scarcity of resources (budget, knowledge), a lack of experience, and other factors. Nevertheless, a combination of strategies is recommended, because, although quick gains are necessary, they should not hamper long-term innovation. As such, innovative business models and information architectures should be developed in parallel to avoid an increase in management costs. This combined approach is an interesting avenue of future research.

Conclusion

Local governments are now faced with the need to transform themselves into smart cities, and they have the ambition to become full-service providers. Rather than merely copying existing solutions, local governments need to embrace new business models and find a match between their business rationale and their information architecture. In this paper, the transformation of local government towards new business models has been explored by analyzing two case studies involving Dutch municipalities eager to adopt the full-service provider business model, in combination with other models, and we have shown that, although end-results may appear to be very similar, they may in fact be based on different configurations of aspects like purpose, value-creating activities, information architecture, resources, involvement of private actors, use of technology, and type of innovation.

The first municipality adopted a citizen-centric approach and managed to adopt new business models within a short time. However, further progress was impaired by the lack of a sound information architecture to facilitate the creation of new business models. Over time, more and more resources were spent on maintaining and controlling the existing architectures rather than using those resources to continue the process of innovation. The second municipality developed an information architecture aimed at implementing an infrastructure that was able to facilitate a number of business models. Although this meant that progress in terms of adopting new business models was initially slower, in the long run the infrastructure facilitated the creation of new business models at lower costs.

The first municipality focused on aligning its business processes with its business strategies by emphasizing the innovation of its front-end, without taking the back-end into account or developing an information architecture. Developments took place on an ad-hoc basis rather than on the basis of a solid information architecture. The existing relationships between subsystems was not scrutinized, and that resulted in a modular type of innovation based on Web 2.0 technologies. This type of innovation is better for the kind of medium-sized municipality we investigated in this case study, which has limited resources. The larger municipality in the second case study has the ambition to build and acquire technological capabilities and prepare its back office for an alignment between its strategy and business models. This type of innovation is based on architecture innovations involving a realignment of the relationships between the various systems by first developing a technology platform and thus creating the conditions for realizing the full-service provider model.

Although in the short term, a front-end approach makes it possible to realize quick gains, it also hampers long-tem developments. On the other hand, the back-end approach realizes hardly any observable advantages for customers. However, in the long run, it may prove to be the better approach, because it offers greater flexibility in terms of creating new business models at relatively low control and maintenance costs. Both case studies demonstrated the way business models and information architectures are connected. Over time, it is information architectures that make it possible to develop new business models.

The primary types of information architectures can be characterized as back-end and front-end integration respectively. Front-end integration can be characterized as user-based integration aimed at externalizing heterogeneous content and data, while back-end integration can be characterized as a semantic and syntactic standardization and integration of resources providing a platform for making information available. Integration is achieved by using a standard platform in which systems can subscribe to certain information elements. The former approach, closely related to Web 2.0 technologies like mashups and widgets, provides flexibility and ad-hoc integration and is an example of modular innovation. In the latter approach, information can not only be externalized, but also used automatically in business processes, which means that it can be viewed as architectural innovation. The two approaches are not mutually exclusive and should be considered complementary. The former approach focuses on interaction between people and computers, whereas the latter approach involves computer-to-computer interaction.

One of the results of this study is that governments should adopt an approach that goes beyond innovating either the front-end or the back-end first. Although quick gains are important, they should not hamper long-term innovation. New business models and supporting information architectures should be developed in parallel with an approach involving both the front-end and the back-end.

Public sector managers should look at their existing IT capabilities when developing their new business models because these capabilities may hamper further improvements. They should have a clear idea what it is they want to achieve with the limited resources at their disposal and select the transformation strategy, business models, and information architecture that helps them realize their ambitions both in the short term and in the long term.

Bibliography

A. Afuah and C.L. Tucci, *Internet Business Models and Strategies* (Boston: McGraw-Hill, Irwin, 2000).

K.V. Andersen and H.Z. Henriksen, "E-Government Maturity Models: Extension of the Layne and Lee Model," *Government Information Quarterly* 23 (2006) 236–248.

F.J. Armour, S.H. Kaisler, and S.Y. Liu, "A Big-Picture Look at Enterprise Architecture," *IEEE IT Professional* 1 (1999) 35–42.

G. Dabinett, "Competing in the Information Age: Urban Regeneration and Economic Development Practices in the City of Sheffield, United Kingdom," *Journal of Urban Technology* 12 (2005) 19–38.

S.A. Hazlett and F. Hill, "E-Government: The Realities of Using IT to Transform the Public Sector," *Managing Service Quality* 13 (2003) 445–452.

J. Hedman and T. Kalling, "The Business Model Concept: Theoretical Underpinnings and Empirical Illustrations," *European Journal of Information Systems* 12 (2003) 49–59.

R.M. Henderson and K.B. Clark, "Architectural Innovation: The Reconfiguration of Existing Product Technologies and the Failure of Established Firms," *Administrative Science Quarterly* 35 (1990) 128–152.

M. Janssen, G. Kuk, and R.W. Wagenaar, "A Survey of Web-Based Business Models for E-Government in the Netherlands," *Government Information Quarterly* 25 (2008) 202–220.

P.W.G. Keen and S. Qureshi, Organizational Transformation through Business Models: A Framework for Business Model Design, paper presented at the 39th *Hawaii International Conference on Information Systems* (Hawaii, USA, 2006)

B. Klievink and M. Janssen, "Realizing Joined-up Government: Dynamic Capabilities and Stage Models for Transformation," *Government Information Quarterly* 26 (2009) 275–284.

G. Kuk, "Digital Divide and Quality of Electronic Service Delivery in UK Local Government," *Government Information Quarterly* 20 (2003) 353–363.

K. Layne and J. Lee, "Developing Fully Functional E-Government: A Four Stage Model," *Government Information Quarterly* 18 (2001) 122–136.

D.S. Linthicum, *Next Generation Application Integration: From Simple Information to Web Services* (Boston: Addison Wesley Professional, 2003).

B. Mahadevan, "Business Models for Internet-Based E-Commerce," *California Management Review* 42 (2000) 55–69.

M. Rappa, Business Models on the Web <http://digitalenterprise.org/models/models.html> (2002) Accessed October 25, 2006

R. Richardson, "Back-Officing Front Office Functions: Organizational and Locational Implications of New Telemediated Services," in *Management of Information and Communication Technologies, Emerging Patterns of Control* (London: ASLIB, 1994), pp. 309–335.

J.W. Ross, "Creating a Strategic IT Architecture Competency: Learning in Stages," *MISQ Quarterly Executive* 2 (2003) 31–43.

M.H. Safizadeh, J.M. Field, and L.P. Ritzman, "An Empirical Analysis of Financial Services Processes with a Front-Office or Back-Office Orientation," *Journal of Operations Management* 21 (2003) 557–576.

H.J. Scholl, "Electronic Government: Information Management Capacity, Organizational Capabilities, and the Sourcing Mix," *Government Information Quarterly* 23 (2006) 73–96.

S.K. Sharma and J.N.D. Gupta, "Building Blocks of an E-Government: A Framework," *Journal of Electronic Commerce in Organizations* 1 (2003) 34–48.

P. Timmers, "Business Models for Electronic Markets," *Electronic Markets* 8 (1998) 3–8.

P. Weill and M. Vitale, *Place to Space: Migrating to E-Business Models* (Harvard: Harvard Business Press, 2001).

P. Weill and M. Vitale, "What IT Infrastructure Capabilities Are Needed to Implement E-Business Models," *MISQ Executive* 1 (2002) 17–34.

J.W.J. Weltevreden, O.A.L.C. Atzema, and R.A. Boschma, "The Adoption of the Internet by Retailers: A New Typology of Strategies," *Journal of Urban Technology* 12 (2005) 59–87.

R.K. Yin, *Case Study Research: Design and Methods* (Newbury Park, CA: Sage Publications, 1989).

J.A. Zachman, "A Framework for Information Systems Architecture," *IBM Systems Journal* 26 (1987) 276–292.

The Triple-Helix Model of Smart Cities: A Neo-Evolutionary Perspective

Loet Leydesdorff and Mark Deakin

ABSTRACT *This paper sets out to demonstrate how the triple-helix model enables us to study the knowledge base of an urban economy in terms of its civil society's support for the evolution of the city as a key component of an innovation system. It argues that cities can be considered as densities in networks among three relevant dynamics: the intellectual capital of universities, the wealth creation of industries, and the democratic government of civil society. It goes on to suggest that these interactions generate dynamic spaces within cities where knowledge can be exploited to bootstrap the technology of regional innovation systems. These dynamic spaces can best be understood as spaces of ubiquitous information and communication technologies (ICT) where knowledge is key to regional innovation systems, creating the notion of "smart cities."*

Introduction

The paper suggests that it is the ability of the university-industry-government dynamic to work as a meta-stabilizing mechanism and reflexive layer in the reinvention of cities that lies behind the surge of academic interest currently being directed at communities. It also suggests the reinvention of cities currently taking place under the so-called "urban renaissance" cannot be defined as a top-level Mode 2 "trans-disciplinary" production of knowledge without a bottom-up cultural reconstruction.

Taking such a "bottom-line" approach to the reinvention of cities, the paper serves to kick-start this cultural reconstruction. This is done by challenging the Mode 2 assumption that such development is the spontaneous product of market economies and by using the critical insights that the triple-helix model offers to represent the policies, academic leadership qualities, and corporate strategies that provide critical insights into the governance of this cultural reconstruction. This reveals that cultural development, however liberal and potentially free, is not a spontaneous product of market economies, but a product of policies that need to be carefully constructed. Otherwise, cultural development of this kind remains merely a series of symbolic events left without the analytical frameworks needed to explain itself in terms of anything but the requirements of the market. This also serves to demonstrate that any such appeal to the efficiency of the market as a means to explain cultural development can only be considered as an analytical shortcut holding back any meaningful specification of the policies that their governance stands on.

Drawing upon the "renaissance" experiences of "world class" cities like Montreal and Edinburgh, the paper provides evidence to show how entrepreneurship-based and market-dependent representations of knowledge production are now being replaced with a community of policy makers, academic leaders, and corporate strategists in alliances that have the potential to liberate cities from the stagnation they have been locked into and offer communities the means to reach beyond the idea of "creative slack" and move towards a process of reinvention that allows cities to become "smarter." Doing this requires cities to use intellectual capital not only to meet the efficiency requirements of wealth creation, but to become centers of creative slack, distinguished by virtue of their communities being not only economically innovative, or culturally creative, but enterprising in opening-up, reflexively absorbing, and discursively shaping the governmental dimensions of this kind of development.

Armed with these critical insights, the neo-evolutionary perspective of the triple-helix model is used as a means to uncover the intellectual capital sustaining the development of cultural reconstruction and reveal how it is possible for this process of reinvention to function as meta-stabilizing mechanisms for integrating cities into the emerging innovation systems.

The Paper

In using the triple-helix model to gain these critical insights into the evolution of smart cities, the paper sub-divides into four sections. The first examines the shift from the so-called "Mode 2" to triple-helix accounts of emerging innovation systems. The second outlines the critical insights surrounding the triple-helix model of knowledge production and cultural reconstruction associated with the notion of smart cities. The third draws upon the triple helix to account for the ongoing reconstruction of Montreal and Edinburgh as smart cities. The examination then goes on to reflect on the critical role this cultural reconstruction of cities, i.e., as smart, takes within regional innovation systems.

From "Mode 2" to Triple Helix: Accounts of Emerging Innovation Systems

The proponents of the "Mode-2" thesis argue that the social system has undergone a radical transition and this has changed the mode of knowledge production. Advocates of the "Mode-2" thesis argue that disciplinary-based knowledge will increasingly become obsolete and should be replaced with techno-scientific knowledge generated in "trans-disciplinary" projects. Within these arguments, the concept of national *systems* of innovations, as it prevails in evolutionary economics, stresses the resilience of existing arrangements.

Extensive research carried out in this tradition has enabled the systematic comparisons of different innovation systems without much questioning of whether nations are the level at which innovation systems are integrated (Lundvall, 1992; Nelson, 1993; Nelson and Winter, 1982). In addition to the idea of the nation-state—as a specific construct of the nineteenth and twentieth centuries—providing a stable context for the development of *national* innovation systems, other scholars have sought to focus on the emergence of *sectorial or regional* systems as potential candidates for the stabilization of interactions among selection environments (Braczyk et al., 1998; Carlsson, 2006; Carlsson and Stankiewicz, 1991).

The triple helix on the other hand, explains these differences among innovation systems at different levels in terms of *possible* arrangements. For example, when the nations of Eastern Europe became transition economies after the demise of the Soviet Union in 1991, the ambitions of these countries to develop national systems of innovation met with interference from market forces, on the one hand, and from the ongoing political process of European accession, on the other. An interesting example of how this worked is provided by the case of Hungary, where not one, but three innovation systems emerged during the transition (Inzelt, 2004).

Here a metropolitan center developed around Budapest to compete with Vienna, Munich, Prague, etc., as a seat for knowledge-intensive services, multinational corporations, etc. In the western part of the country, specific Western-European companies also moved into Hungry and were able to influence research agendas at universities. The German car manufacturer Audi created its own institute at a local university in the North-Western region where it developed an automotive cluster (Lengyel et al., 2006). In addition to this, a third type of innovation system could be detected in the eastern regions, where traditional universities support the development of local infrastructures remaining more continuous with the old system (Lengyel and Leydesdorff, 2011).

This indicated that when Hungary arrived on the European scene, it was too late to develop a purely *national* innovation system because the envisaged system was already implicated in the formation of the European Union. Transition countries became at the same time accession countries for the European Union and the resulting dynamics could, henceforth, only be coordinated loosely at the national level. The period for adaptation was too short for stabilizing a national system of innovations.

The context of the European Union has changed the status of regions, and nation states can be dissolved as in the case of Czechoslovakia, or continuously reformed as in the case of Belgium. Under this regime, each system remains in "endless transition." However, this endless transition does not mean that "anything goes," but rather a continuous recombination of strengths and competitive advantages under selection pressure (Cooke and Leydesdorff, 2006). The selection processes involved are knowledge-intensive because they can only be improved by appreciating the information which becomes available when they operate.

This "disorganization" may vary from country to country and from region to region within countries. In the case of Eastern Europe, the transition not only represents a newly emerging trajectory, but a change in the regime regulating all of this. This "emerging system," however, should not be reified:[1] the interacting *uncertainties* in the distributions determine the dynamics by selecting one another. One can no longer expect a stable center where decision-making can be monopolized because the one-to-one correspondence between functions and institutions no longer prevails. The fragile order of a knowledge base remains a networked order of codified expectations.

The disorganization and fragmentation of previously existing innovation systems is appreciated in the triple-helix model in terms of a reflexive "overlay" of relations among the carriers of innovation systems (Etzkowitz and Leydesdorff, 2000). Here the overlay feeds back as a restructuring sub-dynamic on the underlying networks and generates and/or blocks opportunities for either sectoral, or regional niche-formation in a distributed mode. New competencies may be needed for further developments and new specialties are shaped as a recombination of existing disciplinary capacities. The knowledge-based dynamics are institutionally conditioned, but evolutionary in character: the reflection at the level of the overlay operates from the perspective of hindsight and can, therefore, be future oriented. These dynamics generate flexibilities: not as a biological process of adaptation, but as a *social* dynamic of interactions among meanings, insights, and intentions (Freeman and Perez, 1988; Leydesdorff, 2010, 2011).

The Triple-Helix Model

Unlike the national systems and mode 2 accounts of knowledge production, the triple-helix model:

- studies networks of university-industry-government relations and offers a neo-evolutionary model of a knowledge-based economy
- proposes that the three evolutionary functions shaping the selection environments of a knowledge-based economy are: (i) organized knowledge production, (ii) economic wealth creation, and (iii) reflexive control
- suggests that as reflexivity is always involved as one of them, the functions that they serve are not given, but socially constructed as the inter-human coordination mechanisms of evolving communication systems within given cultural settings.

In a triple-helix model of social coordination, selection dynamics are endogenous because actors in the three institutional spheres relate reflexively. Integration and differentiation among the subsystems are concomitant: the functionally differentiated system is able to process more complexity, while (integrating) exchange relations among the subsystems makes it possible to change perspectives and to develop historically new structures at interfaces. On the one side, one can expect a configuration to be reproduced in which the generation of intellectual capital prevails within an academic environment, with wealth creation being institutionally associated with industry, while control in the public sphere can be associated with government. On the other, network relations can be expected to reflect degrees of integration, for example, in national systems. The degree of integration and whether synergy is generated, however, remain empirical questions that are open to measurement (e.g., Leydesdorff and Fritsch, 2006; Leydesdorff and Sun, 2009).

Under this model, institutions are seen as reacting to each other's selections (Etzkowitz, 2008). The dynamic of this selection process is not biologically inherited (Lewontin, 2000), but cultural, i.e., dependent on the development of communicative competencies (i.e., learning) by the carrying agents. The interactions among the dynamics in the overlay can be intensified by the technologies of information-based communications (ICTs) currently being exploited to generate the notion of "creative cities" (Landry, 2008) and as the knowledge base of "intelligent cities" (Komninos, 2008). Technologies that Hollands (2008) notes are now being asked to become even "smart-er." He explains that he sees the need for technologies to be smarter not just in the way they make it possible for cities to be intelligent (as an institutional agent) in generating capital and creating wealth, but in the ways they operate their governments.

Such a co-evolutionary mechanism for the meta-stabilization of existing institutional arrangements marks a development that takes us beyond the dismantling of national systems and the construction of regional advantages, i.e., those that fall under the remit of "innovations systems" and "Mode-2" accounts. The reinvention of cities currently taking place under the so-called "urban renaissance" cannot be defined as a top-level "trans-disciplinary" issue without a considerable amount of cultural reconstruction at the bottom. Although recognized as important by advocates of the mode-2 perspective, the highly distributed and local character of this reconstruction has to be appreciated as the driver of the transformation.

In our opinion, accounts of this cultural reconstruction have tended to reify the global perspective and fail to appreciate the meta-stabilizing transformations of innovations systematically worked out as the informational content of social and cultural processes operating at the local level. We also suggest that the potential this dynamic has to work as a meta-stabilizing mechanism and reflexive layer is what lies behind the surge of academic interest that is currently focusing on communities as the "practical" manifestation of intellectual capital and exploitation of the knowledge produced from their organization by industrial sectors (Amin and Cohendet, 2004; Amin and Roberts, 2008).

The triple helix, however, distinguishes between the codes of communication operating within these "communities of practice" and highlights the need to specify translation mechanisms among them (Nooteboom, 2008). We suggest that the translations between and among such communications can generate intellectual capital and provide new sources of material for this meta-stabilizing dynamic. For innovation systems can use this knowledge base as a means to counter stagnation and draw upon their networks to develop another—that is, an analytically orthogonal, or third—selection mechanism, which operates between and upon the market forces of institutionally oriented policies. From this perspective, the transformation of "national systems" to the types of conceptual frames outlined in the rest of this paper offers an opportunity for the "nation" to be considered as one among a number of competing hypotheses.

The Ongoing Reconstruction of Montreal and Edinburgh

We suggest under the conceptual frames in question, the decisive level is often not the national but the global stage. For example, cities like Montreal and Edinburgh, although not capital cities in a national innovation system, can obtain the status of "world class" as trans-national city-regions that function as innovation systems. Montreal, for example, has been recognized as a city particularly successful in reinventing itself and developing a "creative" force within the region (Florida, 2004; Slolarick and Florida, 2006). While informal communities are found to generate new knowledge, the city has sought to institutionalize this process of knowledge production by developing into a learning organization. This organizational structure has in turn invented pedagogy by which to integrate knowledge-intensive firms into the metropolitan innovation system. Furthermore, this pedagogy has then developed the means to integrate and exploit these firms as the key components of the emerging innovation system.

As an empirical example, Figure 1 shows the long-term trends in the ratios of patents for Edinburgh and Glasgow (as a sister city), measured on February 15, 2011, in the database of the World Intellectual Property Organization (WIPO) in Geneva. We juxtaposed these results with similar data for Montreal and Calgary as two provincial metropoles in Canada, but in this case using U.S. Patent and Trademark (USPTO) data. Although the industrial and traditional resource

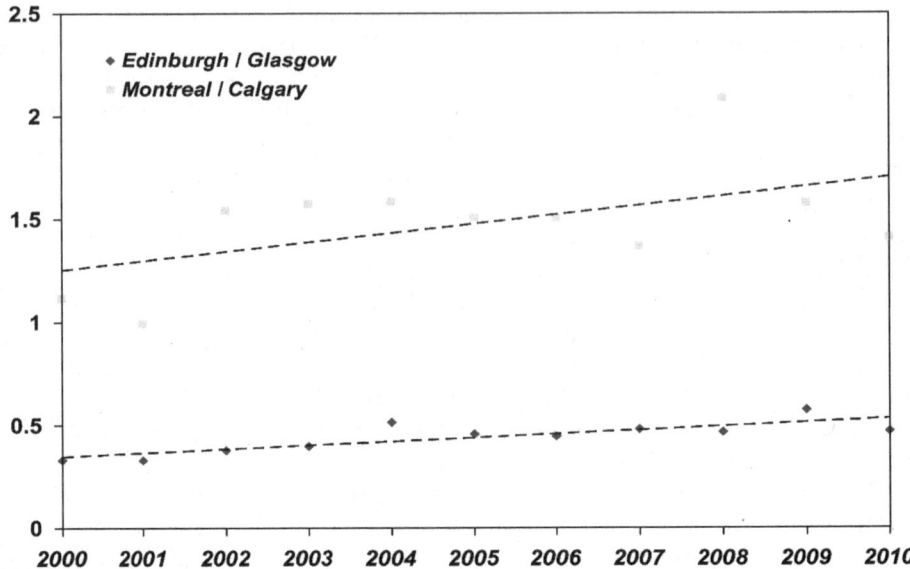

Figure 1. Long-term trends in ratios of patents between Edinburgh versus Glasgow (WIPO data) and Montreal versus Calgary (USPTO data).

bases of both Calgary and Glasgow are much stronger, the patenting in the two smarter cities is slowly gaining ground because of the ongoing transformation from a political economy (organized around the notion of a nation state) to a (globalized) knowledge-based economy.

As Cohendet and Simon (2008) have noted, it is not just universities, industries, or governments, but communities that provide the environments by which it becomes possible for cities to successfully exploit the opportunity to manage integration. For example, the City of Montreal has learned how to become a leading exponent of cultural events, known for the advantage an innovation system manages to construct (Nowotny, 2008). In this case, it might be said, the flow of cultural events into and out of intellectual capital, wealth creation, and the government of civil society interact to open up new windows and perspectives.

The only thing offered to explain the growth of Montreal as a leading exponent of cultural events from the institutional perspective has, however, hitherto been a list of enabling conditions, such as: a strong research and technical development ethic whose shared enterprises are underpinned by leading university involvement. The university involvement is supported by strong leadership from the city and a set of policies capable of governing these ventures as part of an urban regeneration program.

The reduction of these interaction effects among relevant functions to one of the dimensions—contextualizing the other dimensions as mere conditions—tends to lead the discourse towards an economic representation of "innovation systems," or a singularly one-sided account of their scientific and technical qualities from the "trans-disciplinary" perspective of mode-2 knowledge production (Hessels and Van Lente, 2008). In the latter case, the managerial perspective prevails, while in the former, the discourse is economic. However, both discourses fail to unpack the knowledge contents of these socially organized learning processes. The results of science and technology are absorbed as "exogenous fruits from heaven," and the absorption process itself can then not be improved otherwise than by adaptation and imitation.

From our neo-evolutionary perspective, however, these (and other) conditions can be hypothesized as relevant selection environments. The codes operating in these selection environments can be reproduced, adjusted, and strengthened by interacting in local settings. The interactions can be improved by learning how to translate the communication from one context into another.

The Critical Distinction

The critical distinction between the mode-2 type accounts of creative communities, we suggest, set out by the likes of Florida (2004) and Stolarick and Florida (2006), and those of the triple-helix model, lies in the tendency of:

- the former to remain managerial and become locked into neo-liberal policies displaying a strong entrepreneurial legacy, and then to be articulated with reference to the market economy and its regime of accumulation
- the latter to provide a framework for analysis capable of elaborating on what the intellectual capital of universities, the wealth creation of industry, and the government of civil society, each can contribute to the knowledge-intensive policies, academic leadership, and corporate strategies of emerging innovation systems.

Knowledge-intensive polices have to be articulated before they can be exploited through the scientific management of the corporate strategies governing civil society's experience of such developments. Any entrepreneurial drive to by-pass the articulation of these knowledge-intensive polices fails to represent the intellectual capital, wealth creation, and governance invested in cultural constructs (Ramaprasad and Sridhar, 2010).

The triple-helix model allows us to recognize that cultural development, however liberal and potentially free, is not a spontaneous product of market economies, but a product of the policies, academic leadership, and corporate strategies that need to be carefully constructed as part of an urban regeneration program. Müller (2010), for example, showed how Dublin and Gothenburg developed technology parks that were able to innovate a city: one needs to develop a specific and novel understanding—a code—of creativity and the representation of spaces so that knowledge-intensive industries can be embedded in a "creative city." Otherwise, cultural development of this type risks remaining a series of symbolic events, left without the analytical frameworks needed to legitimize itself in terms other than their economic success.

Any such appeal to the efficiency of the market as a means to explain cultural development serves as an analytical shortcut, holding back a more meaningful specification of the policies, leadership qualities, and corporate strategies underpinning an urban regeneration program. For cities like Montreal and Edinburgh show how the creative ecology of an entrepreneurship-based and market-dependent representation of knowledge-intensive firms can be replaced with a learning organization of policy makers, academic leaders, and corporate strategists. These alliances have the potential to liberate cities from the stagnation they have previously been locked into and offer communities the freedom to develop polices capable of reaching beyond the idea of "creative slack" as merely a residual factor. For in order to be more than intelligent and smart, and in that sense, "smarter," cities need the intellectual capital required to not only meet the efficiency requirements of wealth creation under a market economy, but to become centers of creative slack distinguished by virtue of their communities having the political leadership and strategies that are capable of not only being culturally creative, but enterprising in opening-up, reflexively absorbing, and discursively shaping the economic and governmental dimensions of their corporate management.

This neo-evolutionary perspective on the dynamics of learning and their codification of knowledge, can also guide us towards the intellectual capital of such creativity by focusing attention on those dimensions of corporate management that make it possible for urban regeneration programs to function as meta-stabilizing mechanisms that underpin civil society's integration of cities into emerging innovation systems (Deakin and Allwinkle, 2007; Deakin, 2008; 2009). Without cognitive deconstruction and analysis, cultural events, knowledge products, and intellectual achievements run the risk of being reified to little more than signifiers of a market economy. However, a reflexive turn allows the "best practice" examples to be evaluated—instead of imitated—in terms of functional advantages. While there may be no single "best practice" from an evolutionary perspective, this is not critical as long as there is sufficient "slack" in the environment to learn from failures and accommodate alternatives in ways that offer the prospect of self-regenerating actions at the level of the network. The different functionalities this produces can then in turn be articulated into specific policies, informed and further improved by learning from what works and uncovering the reasons why.

Such a critical approach—when compared to the boasting of self-proclaimed "best practices"—challenges policy makers to raise additional questions, such as: whether the university should participate in such an integration, and if so how? What other potentials exist, but have hitherto been insufficiently articulated towards industry? For example: should technologically oriented faculties only be involved, or might this also include the social sciences? These questions arise because here the technology of city-regions surfaces for what they can rightly be considered to be: "nested centers" of control, dependent for their further economic and social development, not only on the market, but on the intellectual capital and wealth creation capabilities of reflexive and self-organizing systems.

Some Reflections

Using the triple-helix model, it can be recognized that cultural development, however liberal and potentially free, is not a spontaneous product of market economics, but a product of the policies which need to be carefully constructed by a governing authority. For:

- cities like Montreal show how the creative ecology of an entrepreneur-based and market-dependent representation of knowledge-intensive firms are currently being replaced with a community of policy makers, academic leaders, and corporate strategists
- these communities in turn have the potential to liberate cities from the stagnation which they have previously been locked into and offer the freedom to develop polices with the leadership and strategies capable of reaching beyond the idea of "creative slack" as a residual factor
- in order for them to be more than intelligent and smart and in that sense, "smarter;" cities need their intellectual capital to not only meet the efficiency requirements of wealth creation under a market economy, but to become

centers of creative slack distinguished by virtue of their communities having the political leadership and strategies capable of not only being culturally creative, but enterprising in using ICT-saturated forms of knowledge-intensive production to open-up, reflexively absorb, and discursively shape the governmental dimensions of their corporate management.

Conclusion

This paper has set out to demonstrate how the triple-helix model enables us to study the knowledge base of an urban economy in terms of civil society's support for the evolution of cities as key components of innovation systems. In this schema, cities can be considered as densities in networks among at least these three relevant dynamics: that is, in the intellectual capital of universities, the industry of wealth creation, and their participation in the democratic government which forms the rule of law in civil society. The effects of these interactions can generate spaces within the dynamics of cities where knowledge production may be exploited. The densities of relations that exist among the spaces of these institutional spheres in turn creates a dynamic which makes it possible for cities to bootstrap the technology of regional innovation systems.

These technologies, we have argued, are enabled by the all-pervasive technologies of information-based communications (ICTs) currently being exploited to generate the notion of "creative cities," as the knowledge base of intelligent cities and their augmentation into smart(er) cities. Such cities are "smarter" at exploiting information and communication technologies and are not only creative or intelligent in generating intellectual capital and creating wealth, but also in selecting environments governing their knowledge production, making them integral parts of emerging innovation systems. The specificity of possible matches is not given, but can be reconstructed, remaining reflexively accessible, knowledge-intensive, and fragile due to the fact that discursive knowledge is based on representations that can be further informed.

This reflexive instability of a knowledge-based system provides the co-evolutionary mechanism between institutional stabilization and communicative meta-stabilization and as such, offers the possibility of relating the city to the "next-order" dynamics in a process of globalization. The capacity to process this transition reflexively, that is, in terms of translations, marks a development that takes us beyond the dismantling of national systems and the construction of regional advantages. Using this neo-evolutionary perspective of the triple-helix model, it can be appreciated that cultural development, however liberal and potentially free, is not a spontaneous product of market economies, but the outcome of policies, academic leadership qualities, and corporate strategies, all of which need to be carefully reconstructed, pieced together, and articulated before management can govern them as requirements of an urban regeneration program.

Note

1. In an e-mail exchange at the CybCom list of the American Society for Cybernetics on June 9, 2010, Klaus Krippendorff argued for abolishing the systems-terminology in the social sciences in favor of the specification of cybernetic mechanisms because the concepts of systems theory tend to connote with reifying or biological metaphors.

Bibliography

A. Amin and P. Cohendet, *Architectures of Knowledge* (Oxon: Oxford Press, 2004).

A. Amin and J. Roberts, "Knowing in Action: Beyond Communities of Practice," *Research Policy* 37:2 (2008) 353–369.

H.J. Braczyk, P. Cooke, and M. Heidenreich, H.J. Braczyk and P. Cooke, eds, *Regional Innovation Systems* (London/Bristol: University College London Press, 1998).

B. Carlsson, "Internationalization of Innovation Systems: A Survey of the Literature," *Research Policy* 35:1 (2006) 56–57.

B. Carlsson and R. Stankiewicz, "On the Nature, Function, and Composition of Technological Systems," *Journal of Evolutionary Economics* 1:2 (1991) 93–118.

P. Cohendet and L. Simon, "Knowledge-Intensive Firms, Communities, and Creative Cities," in A. Amin and J. Roberts, eds., *Community, Economic Creativity, and Organization* (Oxon: Oxford University Press, 2008).

P. Cooke and L. Leydesdorff, "Regional Development in the Knowledge-Based Economy: The Construction of Advances," *Journal of Technology Transfer* 31:1 (2006) 5–15.

M. Deakin, "The IntelCities Community of Practice: The eGov Services Model for Socially-Inclusive and Participatory Urban Regeneration Programs," in C. Reddick, ed., *A Handbook of Research on Strategies for Local E-Government Adoption and Implementation: Comparative Studies* (Hershey: IGI Global, 2009).

M. Deakin, "The Search for Sustainable Communities: Ecological-Integrity, Equity, and the Question of Participation," in R. Vreeker, M. Deakin, and S. Curwell, eds., *Sustainable Urban Development: Volume 3 – The Toolkit for Assessment* (Oxon: Routledge, 2008).

M. Deakin and S. Allwinkle, "Urban Regeneration and Sustainable Communities: The Role of Networks, Innovation, and Creativity in Building Successful Partnerships," *Journal of Urban Technology* 14:1 (2007) 77–91.

H. Etzkowitz, *The Triple Helix: University-Industry-Government Innovation in Action* (London: Routledge, 2008).

H. Etzkowitz and L. Leydesdorff, "The Dynamics of Innovation: From National Systems and 'Mode 2' to a Triple Helix of University-Industry-Government Relations," *Research Policy* 29:2 (2000) 109–123.

R. Florida, *The Rise of the Creative Class: A Toolkit for Urban Innovators* (New York: Basic Books, 2004).

C. Freeman and C. Perez, "Structural Crises of Adjustment, Business Cycles, and Investment Behavior," in G. Dosi, C. Freeman, R. Nelson, G. Silverberg, and L. Soete, eds., *Technical Change and Economic Theory* (London: Pinter, 1988).

L. Hessels and H. van Lente, "Re-thinking New Knowledge Production: A Literature Review and Research Agenda," *Research Policy* 37:4 (2008) 740–760.

R. Hollands, "Will the Real Smart City Stand Up? Intelligent, Progressive, or Entrepreneirual?"," *City* 12:3 (2008) 302–320.

A. Inzelt, "The Evolution of University-Industry-Government Relationships During Transition," *Research Policy* 33:6/7 (2004) 975–995.

N. Komninos, *Intelligent Cities and Globalization of Innovation Networks* (London: Taylor & Francis, 2008).

C. Landry, *The Creative Center* (London: Earthscan, 2008).

B. Lengyel and L. Leydesdorff, "Regional Innovation Systems in Hungary: The Failing Synergy at the National Level," *Regional Studies* 45:5 (2011) 677–693.

B. Lengyel, E. Lukács, and G. Solymári, "A Külföldi Erdekeltségű Vállalkozások és az Sgyetemek Kapcsolata Győrött, Miskolcon és Szegeden," *Tér és Társadalom* 4 (2006) 127–140.

R. Lewontin, *The Triple Helix: Gene, Organism, and Environment* (Cambridge MA/London: Harvard University Press, 2000).

L. Leydesdorff, "'Meaning' as a Sociological Concept: A Review of the Modelling, Mapping and Simulation of the Communication of Knowledge and Meaning," *Social Science Information* 50: 3–4 (2011) 1–23.

L. Leydesdorff, "The Communication of Meaning and the Structuration of Expectations: Giddens Structuration Theory and Luhmann's Self-Organization," *Journal of the American Society for Information Science and Technology* 61:10 (2010) 2138–2150.

L. Leydesdorff, "The Non-Linear Dynamics of Meaning-Processing in Social Systems," *Social Science Information* 48:1 (2009) 5–33.

L. Leydesdorff and M. Fritsch, "Measuring the Knowledge Base of Regional Innovation Systems in Germany in Terms of a Triple-Helix Dynamic," *Research Policy* 35:10 (2006) 1538–1553.

L. Leydesdorff and Y. Sun, "National and International Dimensions of the Triple Helix in Japan: University-Industry-Government Versus International Co-Authorship Relations," *Journal of the American Society for Information Science and Technology* 60:4 (2009) 778–788.

B.A. Lundvall, *National Systems of Innovation* (London: Pinter, 1992).

A.L. Müller, "Creative Cities as Built Places of the Knowledge Society," paper presented at the *8th International Conference of the Triple Helix of University-Industry-Government Relations* (Madrid, October 20–22, 2010)

R.R. Nelson, *National Innovation Systems: A Comparative Analysis* (New York: Oxford University Press, 1993).

R.R. Nelson and S.G. Winter, *An Evolutionary Theory of Economic Change* (Cambridge, MA: Belknap Press of Harvard University Press, 1982).

B. Nooteboom, "Cognitive Distance between Communities of Practice and in Firms," in A. Amin and J. Roberts, eds., *Community, Economic Creativity and Organization* (Oxon: Oxford University Press, 2008).

H. Nowotny, *Insatiable Curiosity: Innovation in a Fragile Future* (Cambridge, MA: MIT Press, 2008).

A. Ramaprasad and M. K. Sridhar, "Empowering a State's Development of a Knowledge Society," paper presented at the *8th International Conference of the Triple Helix of University-Industry-Government Relations* (Madrid, October 20–22, 2010)

K. Stolarick and R. Florida, "Creativity, Connectivity, and Connections: The Case of Montreal," *Environment and Planning A* 38 (2006) 1779–1817.

Smart Cities in Europe

Andrea Caragliu, Chiara Del Bo, and Peter Nijkamp

ABSTRACT *Urban performance currently depends not only on a city's endowment of hard infrastructure (physical capital), but also, and increasingly so, on the availability and quality of knowledge communication and social infrastructure (human and social capital). The latter form of capital is decisive for urban competitiveness. Against this background, the concept of the "smart city" has recently been introduced as a strategic device to encompass modern urban production factors in a common framework and, in particular, to highlight the importance of Information and Communication Technologies (ICTs) in the last 20 years for enhancing the competitive profile of a city.*

The present paper aims to shed light on the often elusive definition of the concept of the "smart city." We provide a focused and operational definition of this construct and present consistent evidence on the geography of smart cities in the EU27. Our statistical and graphical analyses exploit in depth, for the first time to our knowledge, the most recent version of the Urban Audit data set in order to analyze the factors determining the performance of smart cities. We find that the presence of a creative class, the quality of and dedicated attention to the urban environment, the level of education, and the accessibility to and use of ICTs for public administration are all positively correlated with urban wealth. This result prompts the formulation of a new strategic agenda for European cities that will allow them to achieve sustainable urban development and a better urban landscape.

Introduction

What is the source of urban growth and of sustainable urban development? This question has received continuous attention from researchers and policy makers for many decades. Cities all over the world are in a state of flux and exhibit complex dynamics. As cities grow, planners devise "complex systems to deal with food supplies on an international scale, water supplies over long distances, and local waste disposal, urban traffic management systems, and so on; (...) and the quality of all such urban inputs defines the quality of life of urban dwellers" (The Science Museum, 2004).

Notwithstanding the enormous formidable challenges and disadvantages associated with urban agglomerations, the world population has been steadily concentrating in cities. Figure 1 shows the percentage of EU citizens living in cities (population living in areas classified as urban according to the country-specific criteria selected by the UN); a massive rise in this percentage took place, from slightly more than 50 percent in 1950 to more than 75 percent of EU

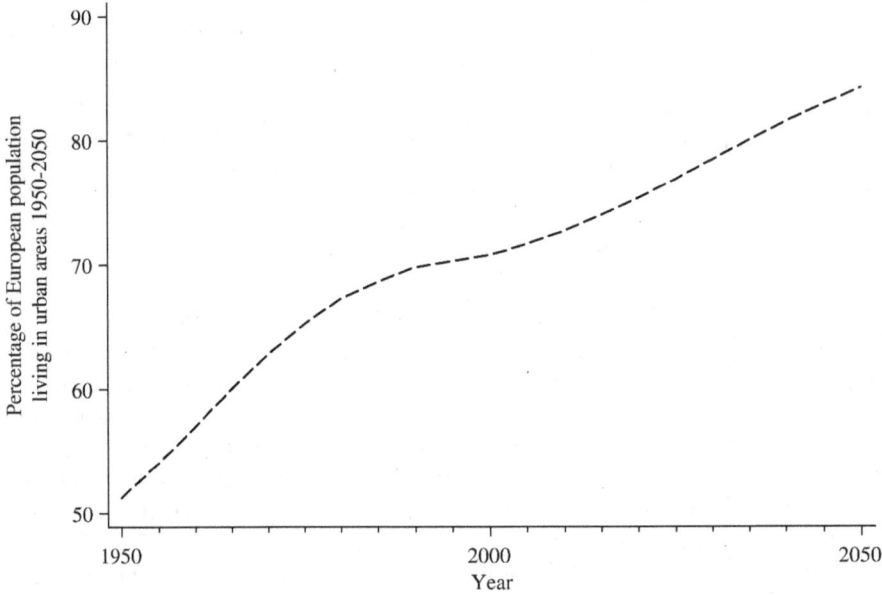

Figure 1. Percentage of EU population living in urban areas, 1950-2050 (forecast)
Source: UN (2009)

population being located in urban areas in the year 2010, and a forecast of about 85 percent within the next 40 years.

In addition, we have also witnessed a substantial increase in the average size of urban areas. This has been made possible by a simultaneous upward shift in the urban technological frontier so that a city can accommodate more inhabitants. Problems associated with urban agglomerations have usually been solved by means of creativity, human capital, cooperation (sometimes bargaining) among relevant stakeholders, and bright scientific ideas: in a nutshell, "smart" solutions. The label "smart city" should, therefore, point to clever solutions allowing modern cities to thrive, through quantitative and qualitative improvements in productivity. However, when googling "smart city definition,"[1] we discovered that included among the very first results were links to a communications provider, a U.S. radio station, an Edinburgh hostel, an initiative of the Amsterdam Innovation Engine, and so on; but no sign of a proper definition.

In the present paper we search for a clear and focused definition of the term "smart city." We next provide qualitative evidence on the correlations between the dimensions of our definition of smart cities and a measure of wealth, i.e., per capita GDP in Purchasing Power Parity (henceforth, PPP).[2] We will start with a brief literature review in the next section.

Literature Review

The concept of the smart city has been quite fashionable in the policy arena in recent years. Its main focus seems to be on the role of ICT infrastructure, although much research has also been carried out on the role of human capital/education, social and relational capital, and environmental interest as important drivers of urban growth.

The European Union, in particular, has devoted constant efforts to devising a strategy for achieving urban growth in a "smart" way for its metropolitan areas. Not only the European Union, but also other international institutions and think tanks believe in a wired, ICT-driven form of development. The Intelligent Community Forum, for example, produces research on the local effects of the ICT revolution, which has now spread worldwide. The OECD and EUROSTAT *Oslo Manual* (2005) stresses the role of innovation in ICT sectors and provides a toolkit to identify consistent indicators, thus shaping a sound framework of analysis for researchers on urban innovation. At a *meso*-regional level, we observe renewed attention to the role of soft communication infrastructure in determining economic performance.[3]

The availability and quality of the ICT infrastructure is not the only definition of a smart or *i*ntelligent city. Without reference to the "smartness" concept, the relation between ICT infrastructure and economic performance has been the object of a flourishing literature since the beginning of the digital era (e.g., Roller and Waverman, 2001). Other definitions stress the role of human capital and education in urban development. Berry and Glaeser (2005) and Glaeser and Berry (2006) show, for example, that the most rapid urban growth rates have been achieved in cities where an educated labor force is available. In particular Berry and Glaeser (2005) model the relation between human capital and urban development by assuming that innovation is driven by entrepreneurs who innovate in industries and products that require an increasingly more skilled labor force.

As not all cities are equally successful in investing in human capital, the educated labor force—or, in Florida's jargon, the "creative class"—is spatially clustering over time. This recognized tendency of cities to have different levels of human capital has attracted the attention of researchers and policy makers. It turns out that cities that had a skilled labor force in the past are able to attract more skilled labor in the present than competing cities. Policy makers, in particular European ones, are most likely to attach a consistent weight to spatial homogeneity; in these circumstances the progressive clustering of urban human capital is a major concern.

An interesting contribution (Fu, 2007) relates the smartness concept to the generation of localized knowledge spillovers (LKS). In this paper, human capital externalities originate from face-to-face contacts between peers in an urban environment. This paper follows the traditional literature on LKS, which encompasses Rauch (1993). Recent and valuable critical reviews of the concept of LKS can be found in Breschi and Lissoni (2001) and in Capello (2009).

The label "smart city" is still, in our opinion, quite a fuzzy concept. Hollands (2008) stresses this point while also providing several examples of self-defined smart cities. In this paper, we move forward by adding a critical review of the literature on smart urban growth from an economist's perspective and an exploratory empirical analysis. With this aim, we summarize the characteristics proper to a smart city that tend to be common to many of the previous findings as follows:

1. The "*utilization of networked infrastructure to improve economic and political efficiency and enable social, cultural, and urban development*," (Hollands, 2008: 308) where the term "infrastructure" indicates business services, housing, leisure, and lifestyle services, and ICTs (mobile and fixed phones, computer networks, e-commerce, and Internet services). This point brings to the forefront the idea of

a wired city as the main development model and of connectivity as the source of growth.

2. *An "underlying emphasis on business-led urban development"* (Hollands, 2008: 308). According to several critiques of the concept of the smart city, this idea of neo-liberal urban spaces, where business-friendly cities would aim to attract new businesses, would be misleading. However, although caveats on the potential risks associated with putting an excessive weight on economic values as the sole driver of urban development may be worth noting, the data actually shows that business-oriented cities are indeed among those with a satisfactory socio-economic performance.

3. *A strong focus on the aim of achieving the social inclusion of various urban residents in public services* (e.g., Southampton's smartcard; see Southampton City Council 2006). This prompts researchers and policy makers to give attention to the crucial issue of equitable urban growth. In other words: To what extent do all social classes benefit from a technological integration of their urban fabric?

4. *A stress on the crucial role of high-tech and creative industries in long-run urban growth.* This factor, along with "soft infrastructure" ("knowledge networks, voluntary organizations, crime-free environments, after dark entertainment economy"), is the core of Richard Florida's research. The basic idea in this case is that "creative occupations are growing and firms now orient themselves to attract "the 'creative'" (Hollands, 2008: 309). Employers now prod their hires onto greater bursts of inspiration. The urban lesson of Florida's book is that cities that want to succeed must aim at attracting the creative types who are, Florida argues, the wave of the future" (Glaeser, 2005: 593). The role of creative cultures in cities is also critically summarized in Nijkamp (2008), where creative capital co-determines, fosters, and reinforces trends of skilled migration. While the presence of a creative and skilled workforce does not guarantee urban performance, in a knowledge-intensive, and increasingly, globalized economy, these factors increasingly will determine the success of cities.

5. *Profound attention to the role of social and relational capital in urban development.* A smart city will be a city whose community has learned to learn, adapt, and innovate (Coe et al., 2001). People need to be able to use technology in order to benefit from it: this refers to the absorptive capacity literature. This concept has been applied to different economic relations at different levels of spatial aggregation. The basic reference is Cohen and Levinthal (1990); Abreu et al. (2008) bridges the idea from a micro-, firm level to a more aggregated, meso-level; finally, Caragliu and Nijkamp (2011) test the role of regional absorptive capacity in inducing spatial knowledge spillovers.

When social and relational issues are not properly taken into account, social polarization may arise as a result. This last issue is also linked to economic, spatial, and cultural polarization. It should be noted, however, that some research actually argues the contrary. Poelhekke (2006), for example, shows that the concentration of high skilled workers is conducive to urban growth, irrespective of the polarization effects that this process may generate at a *meso-* (for example, regional) level. The debate on the possible class inequality effects of policies oriented towards creating smart cities is, however, still not resolved.

6. *Finally, social and environmental sustainability as a major strategic component of smart cities.* In a world where resources are scarce and where cities are increasingly basing their development and wealth on tourism and natural resources,

their exploitation must guarantee the safe and renewable use of natural heritage. This last point is linked to the third item, because the wise balance of growth-enhancing measures, on the one hand, and the protection of weak links, on the other, is a cornerstone for sustainable urban development.

Items 5 and 6 are for us the most interesting and promising ones from both a research and a policy perspective; we believe, therefore, that they may represent the object of future research for urban economists. In the next sections we provide quantitative and analytical evidence of the role of the creative class and human capital in sustainable urban development, arguing that it is indeed the mix of these two dimensions that determine the very notion of a smart city. The relational capital side of the story is not evaluated in the present paper, but this will be the subject of further research in future studies.

Along with the previously mentioned critical points, additional critiques have been advanced to question the concept of a smart or intelligent city. Hollands (2008) provides a thorough treatment of the main arguments against the superficial use of this concept in the policy arena. His main points are the following:

- The focus of the concept of smart city may lead to an underestimation of the possible negative effects of the development of the new technological and networked infrastructures needed for a city to be smart (on this topic, see also Graham and Marvin, 1996).
- This bias in strategic interest may lead to ignoring alternative avenues of promising urban development.
- Among these possible development patterns, policy makers would better consider those that depend not only on a business-led model. As a globalized business model is based on capital mobility, following a business-oriented model may result in a losing long-term strategy: "The 'spatial fix' inevitably means that mobile capital can often 'write its own deals' to come to town, only to move on when it receives a better deal elsewhere. This is no less true for the smart city than it was for the industrial, manufacturing city" (Hollands, 2008:314).

From a U.S. perspective, research on smart cities has also evaluated the relevance of smart urban development in fighting urban sprawl (Bronstein, 2009); used a cognitive approach in assessing the role of psychological and cognitive attitudes towards ICTs in reducing the extent of the digital divide (Partridge, 2004); and verified on the field (through a case study on a community project) whether concrete action can be taken against such a digital divide in poor urban areas (Mc Allister et al., 2005).

Our paper will now provide some quantitative evidence on many of these points, supported by spatial statistics, maps, and graphical evidence on each of the points that the literature on smart cities has put forward in order to explore and identify statistical correlations with socioeconomic urban performance.

An Operational Definition of the Smart City

A narrow definition of a much-used concept may help in understanding the scope of the present paper. Although several different definitions of smart city have been given in the past, most of them focus on the role of communication infrastructure. However, this bias reflects the time period when the smart city label gained interest, viz. the early 1990s, when ICTs first reached a wide audience in European countries. Hence, in our opinion, the stress on the Internet as "the" smart city identifier no longer suffices.

A recent and interesting project conducted by the Centre of Regional Science at the Vienna University of Technology identifies six main "axes" (dimensions) along which a ranking of 70 European middle size cities can be made. These axes are: a smart economy; smart mobility; a smart environment; smart people; smart living; and, finally, smart governance. These six axes connect with traditional regional and neoclassical theories of urban growth and development. In particular, the axes are based—respectively—on theories of regional competitiveness, transport and ICT economics, natural resources, human and social capital, quality of life, and the participation of society members in cities. We believe this offers a solid background for our theoretical framework, and, therefore, we base our definition on these six axes.

We believe a city to be smart when investments in human and social capital and traditional (transport) and modern (ICT) communication infrastructure fuel sustainable economic growth and a high quality of life, with a wise management of natural resources, through participatory governance.

Quantitative and Graphical Evidence on European Smart Cities

In this section we will present graphical and quantitative evidence on the relative performance and rankings of European cities with respect to measures reflecting some of the definitions of a smart city given in the literature. The data source is the Urban Audit data set in its latest wave (2003-2006). The Urban Audit entails a collection of comparable statistics and indicators for European cities; it contains data for over 250 indicators across the following domains:

- demography
- social aspects
- economic aspects
- civic involvement
- training and education
- environment
- travel and transport
- information society
- culture and recreation.

Cities that were surveyed in the latest available wave are depicted in Map 1.

We now present a set of charts which show partial correlations between urban growth determinants and our measure of economic output, which is per capita GDP in purchasing power standards (PPS) in 2004 (the latest data available in the Urban Audit data set). For the sake of readability, cities are indicated with their Urban Audit code. (A complete correspondence table is available as an Appendix to this paper.)

The set of all partial correlations among the variables we use to measure the "smartness" of European cities can be found in Table 1, with corresponding p-values in parentheses. It is evident that most of the variables that we deem as capable of both co-determining long-run urban performance and characterizing a thorough definition of smart city tend to be positively associated with our measure of urban wealth (we chose per capita GDP in PPS in 2004 in order to avoid the problem of size effects and to take into account price differentials

Map 1. Cities in the 2003-2006 Urban Audit survey

Table 1: Partial correlations among the six indicators of Smart Cities

	Per Capita GDP in PPS	Employment in the Entertainment Industry	Multimodal Accessibility	Length of Public Transport Network	e-Government	Human Capital
Per Capita GDP in PPS	1					
Employment in the Entertainment Industry	0.215 (0.1258)	1				
Multimodal Accessibility	0.7049 0	−0.0059 (0.9553)	1			
Length of Public Transport Network	0.3104 (0.0043)	0.2874 (0.0302)	0.0919 (0.312)	1		
e-Government	0.1418 (0.1751)	−0.0254 (0.8385)	0.141 (0.1004)	−0.0339 (0.7417)	1	
Human Capital	−0.1361 (0.265)	−0.0983 (0.3649)	0.0833 (0.3616)	−0.0741 (0.5946)	0.0665 (0.5733)	1

Note: p-values are in parentheses

across countries, which might be particularly different among EU15 and New Member State [NMS] cities). An interesting but puzzling result arises for the relationship between the level of education of people living in our sample and their average individual income; this issue will be further analyzed later in this section. Throughout this section, on the map as well as in our charts, we indicate the code of the city associated with each observation. We believe this to be a useful tool of analysis for both researchers and policymakers, allowing them to identify intriguing spatial issues in the Urban Audit data set, to note the possible presence of country effects, and to identify the locational patterns of our smart city measures.

Figure 2 offers partial support for Richard Florida's arguments on the role of the "creative class" in determining long-run urban performance. Positive correlations between the share of people employed in a "creative" industry (Florida, 2002; 2009), and in particular in the "super-creative core," are found in U.S. cities and states. In Florida (2002) the creative class is defined as the merger of two Standard Occupational Classification System codes within the U.S. labor force, viz.:

- A super-creative core with those employed in science, engineering, education, computer programming, research, and with arts, design, and media workers making a small subset. Those belonging to this group are considered to "fully engage in the creative process" (Florida, 2002: 69).
- Creative professionals with those employed in healthcare, business and finance, the legal sector, and education.

Here, we measure these effects with the share of the labor force in European cities in the culture and entertainment industry and find, indeed, that the two measures show a positive and significant correlation (the correlation coefficient equals .2150 with a p-value of .1258).

In the urban economics literature, Florida's view has not been exempt from criticism (Glaeser, 2005). In the opinion of several economists, the argument that the creative professions would drive urban performance is flawed, and it would

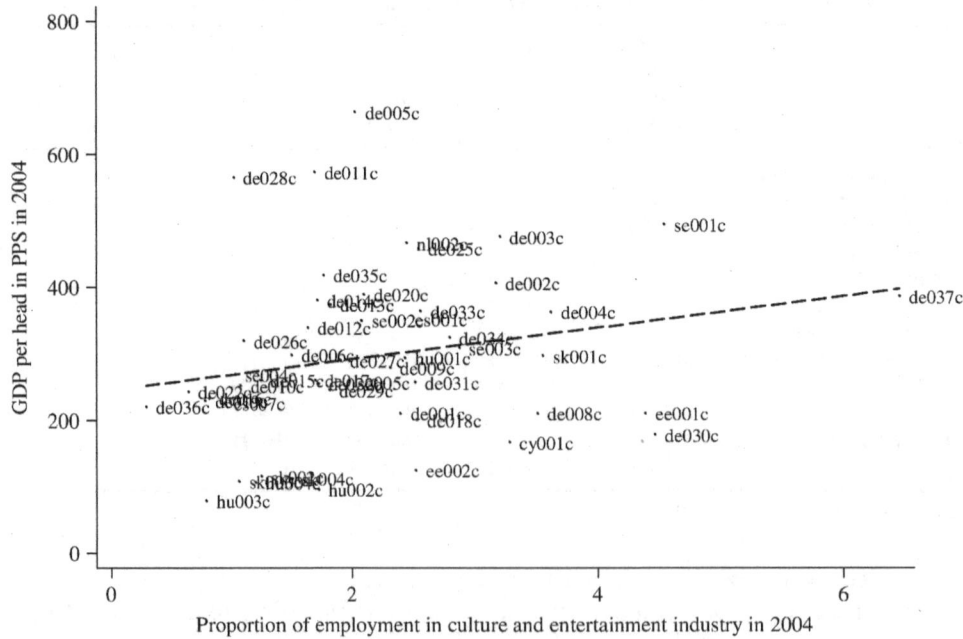

Figure 2. Creative class and wealth in 2004

only be a proxy for the role of the "hard" measurable stock of human capital (i.e., technical professions and total years of schooling) on urban growth. Shapiro (2008) provides an excellent and convincing bridge between the two views. In his paper, he proves with careful econometric estimations that human capital in cities contributes both directly to urban growth (measured by the growth of population, wages, and two land-rent measures) through productivity gains and indirectly through the increase in urban amenities, which in turn may foster the process of attraction of the creative class. Although the productivity effects are still the largest, according to Shapiro's estimates, the amenities effects would account for as much as 20 to 30 percent of total human capital effects on urban growth.

A second positive (and extremely significant) correlation appears to exist between multimodal accessibility and per capita GDP. (See Figure 3.) The multimodal accessibility index is based on the assumption that the attraction of a destination increases with its size (in terms of population and GDP) and declines with distance, travel time, and costs (which in turn lays its foundations in gravitational models of trade). Values of the index oscillate around 100, which is the average for the EU27. In this chart, the accessibility indicator, calculated as a weighted average of the ease with which a city can be reached with a combined set of available transportation modes (i.e., rail, road, sea, or plane), also represents a measure for the market potential available to and from the city itself. Therefore, a better endowment of transportation means might be conducive to wealth and growth; this last statement being in line with the New Economic Geography's theoretical expectations. A good example of the role of the market potential in driving economic performance in the New Economic Geography literature can be found in Redding and Sturm (2008), who in turn follow the rich tradition encompassing, among many, Davis and Weinstein (2003) and Hanson (2005).

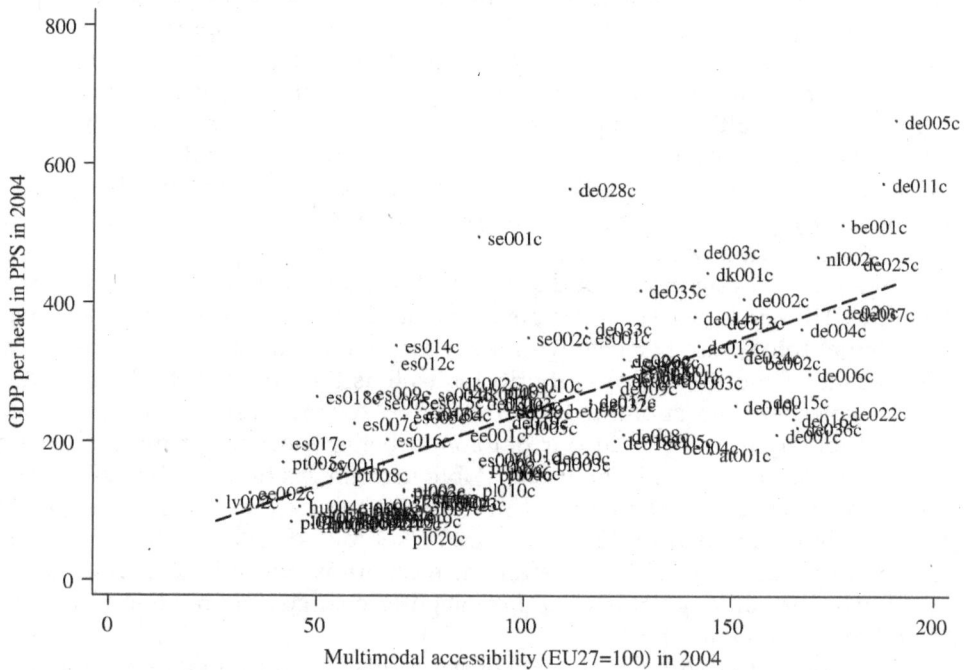

Figure 3. Accessibility and wealth in 2004

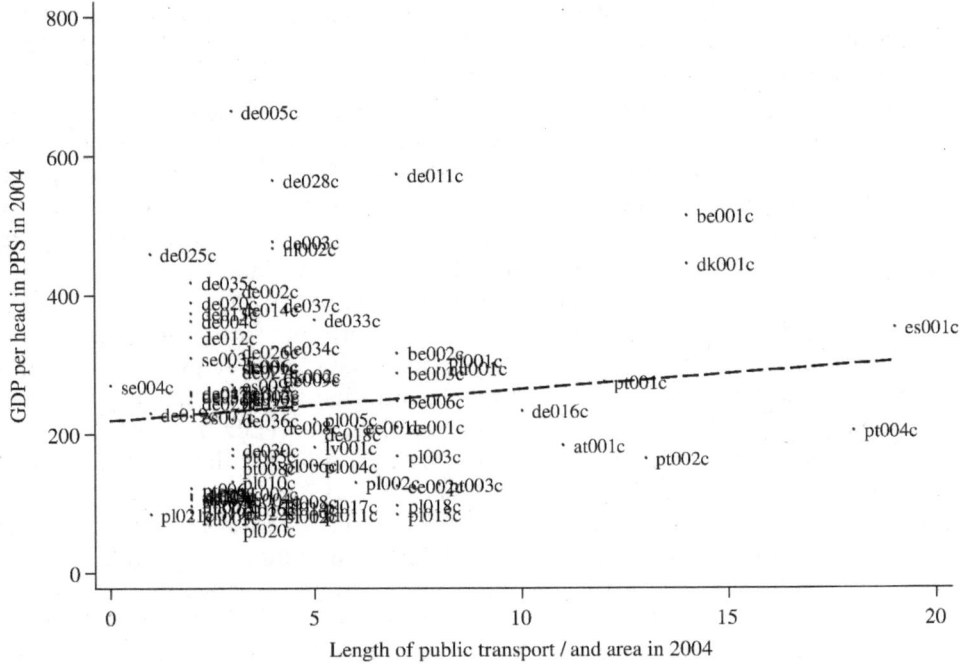

Figure 4. Public transport and wealth

Figure 4 shows instead the relationship between the availability of public transportation (normalized by the city area) and the level of wealth, measured as before with per capita GDP in PPS. The relationship is strongly positive; the city of Stockholm has been excluded from the original dataset as it behaves as an outlier, with an outstandingly high density of public transportation. With the inclusion of Stockholm the interpolation line would become even steeper. It is quite evident that an efficient net of public transportation is associated with high levels of wealth. Although the direction of causality in this relation may go both ways, it seems reasonable to think that a dense public transportation network may help to reverse the negative effects of urban density, thus at least partly releasing the pressure this exerts on the urban landscape and reducing the costs associated with congestion.

A slightly less significant and less steep association can be found between the level of GDP and a measure of e-government. The Urban Audit data set yields both the absolute number of government forms that can be downloaded from the website of the municipal authority, as well as the number of administrative forms which can be submitted electronically. As this last series has slightly more observations, and is, in our opinion, a better measure of the real chance for citizens to interact with the urban Public Administration via the net, we represent this in Figure 5. The city of Krakow is in this case excluded as an outlier (in terms of the number of forms that can be submitted online). The relationship does not change when the e-government measure is normalized by population or labor force (although this operation slightly changes the relative ranking of the cities in our sample).

Although cities with a high level of per capita GDP also tend to devote more attention to smart, e-government solutions, it is interesting to observe that some

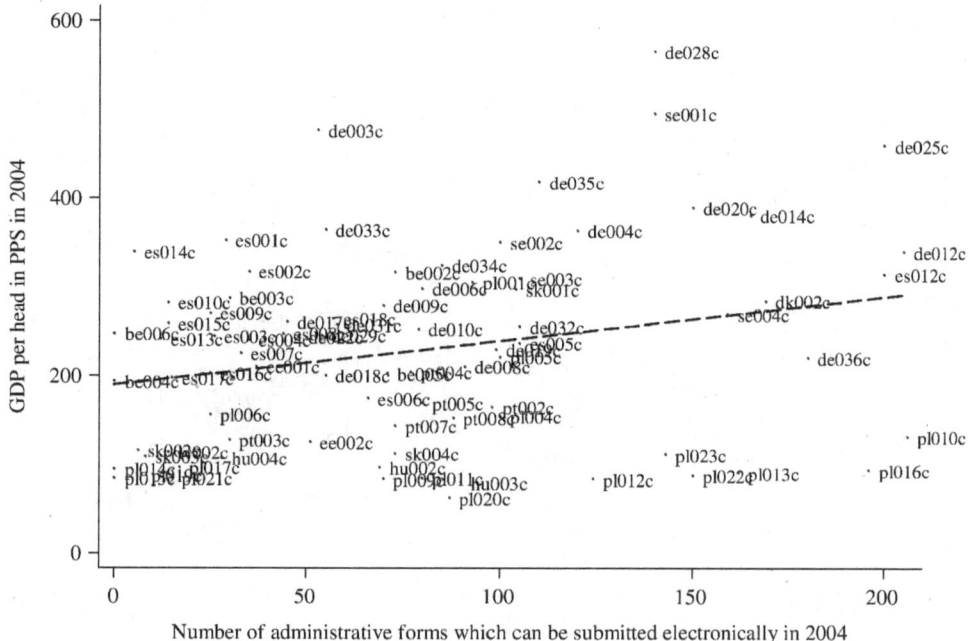

Figure 5. e-Government and wealth

noticeable exceptions characterize this analysis. Some cities in peripheral countries (Krakow in Poland; Zaragoza in Spain; Ponto Delgada in Portugal) have also devised a wide set of forms that citizens can submit online, thus reducing travel and commuting costs, and costs associated with the management of multi-task public administration bodies.

Finally, Figure 6 shows the relationship between the stock of human capital and the level of urban wealth. According to neoclassical theories (Lucas, 1988; Arrow, 1962; Mankiw et al., 1992), human capital levels are good predictors of subsequent economic performance. As Table 1 shows, in our sample this positive relationship has, nevertheless, more complex characteristics. The correlation coefficient between our measure of human capital, i.e., the share of the labor force qualified at ISCED levels 3 and 4, and the level of GDP is negative (although not significant at any statistical confidence level). The International Standard Classification of Education (ISCED) was designed by UNESCO in the early 1970s to serve "as an instrument suitable for assembling, compiling and presenting statistics of education both within individual countries and internationally." It was approved by the International Conference on Education (Geneva, 1975) and was subsequently endorsed by UNESCO's General Conference when it adopted the Revised Recommendation concerning the International Standardization of Educational Statistics at its twentieth session (Paris, 1978) (Unesco, 2006).

Does this imply that more education is associated with poorer economic conditions? If we look at Figure 6 it seems clear that the correct fit of this relationship is through a quadratic interpolation. After an appropriate (quadratic) term has been taken into account, the linear correlation between human capital and GDP is positive and significant at the 1 percent level.[4]

The interpretation of this finding is, however, more difficult. By examining Figure 6 it is possible to identify some observations on the right-hand side of

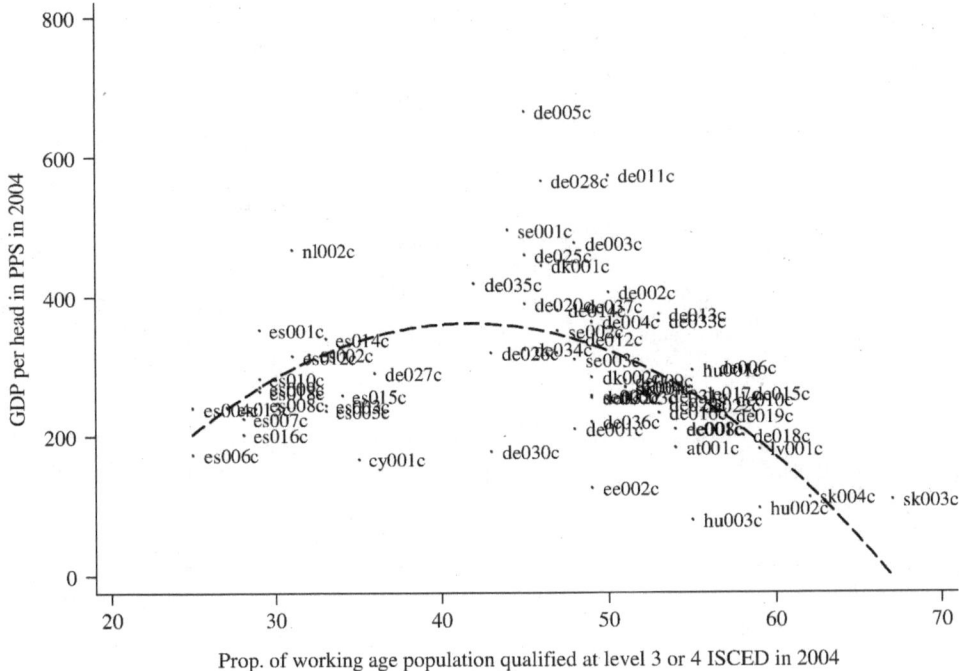

Figure 6. Human capital and wealth

the chart as cities in the NMS of the EU. As a legacy of the Communist period, when levels of education were deliberately held high, labor forces in those countries may still own a large stock of human capital, although overall levels of individual wealth may not yet match those of the old Member States. In this case, therefore, the depicted relationship may actually represent an off-saddle growth path portrait of the real human capital-urban growth equation. Indirect evidence to support this guess comes from splitting the sample into countries that in the 1980s were liberal or "capitalist" in Europe and those which belonged to COMECON, and then fitting the data with a linear trend; the latter turns out to be positive and significant for the first of these two subsamples and negative and significant for the second.

A second key to interpreting the puzzle may be obtained by reconnecting our study to Mayer (2007). She analyzes the different ways in which cities and regions can set up a high-technology cluster even without the presence of a sound research-oriented university, while also criticizing the opposite side of the story, viz. the idea that academic research centers are a necessary and sufficient condition for achieving high-tech oriented urban development. Therefore, cities in NMS may still fail to provide a sound connection between academic research institutes and the real economy, thus failing to attract the human capital-rich workers who raise productivity and wealth.

Conclusions and Policy Implications

In this paper, we have presented an overview of the concept of the smart city, with a critical review of the previous economics and planning approaches to this concept. We then presented a narrower definition of the concept of the smart city, and reviewed some quantitative and graphical evidence on the correlations of some of the main determinants of economic performance and the most important measure of urban success, viz. per capita wealth.

Data from the 2004 Urban Audit data set show consistent evidence of a positive association between urban wealth and the presence of a vast number of creative professionals, a high score in a multimodal accessibility indicator, the quality of urban transportation networks, the diffusion of ICTs (most noticeably in the e-government industry), and, finally, the quality of human capital. These positive associations clearly define a policy agenda for smart cities, although clarity does not necessarily imply ease of implementation.

All variables shown to be positively associated with urban growth can be conceived of as stocks of capital; they are accumulated over time and are subject to decay. Hence, educating people is on average successful only when investment in education is carried out over a long period with a stable flow of resources; transportation networks must be constantly updated to keep up with other fast-growing cities, in order to keep attracting people and ideas; the fast pace of innovation in the ICT industry calls for a continuous and deep restructuring and rethinking of the communication infrastructure, to prevent European cities from losing ground to global competitors.

This continuous challenge, the "endless frontier" to quote Vannevar Bush's words on scientific research (Bush, 1945), is the only way to ensure a sustainable path of development for cities, while at the same time guaranteeing that cities will maintain their crucial role as the cradle of ideas and freedom.

Notes

1. This Google search was carried out on April 8, 2009.
2. PPP methods make it possible to better represent spatial disparities in the level of prices, and, consequently, more accurately gauge the real spending power of economic agents.
3. Del Bo and Florio (2008) offer a critical perspective on previous studies regarding the role of different forms of infrastructure in economic performance and provide empirical evidence on the contribution of single and aggregate measures of infrastructure on regional growth in the period 1995-2005.
4. Evidence of this last finding is available from the authors upon request.

Bibliography

M. Abreu, V. Grinevich, M. Kitson, and M. Savona, "Absorptive Capacity and Regional Patterns of Innovation," *Research Report* 8/11 (London: Department of Innovation, Universities, and Skills, 2008).

K.J. Arrow, "The Economic Implications of Learning By Doing," *Review of Economic Studies* 29:3 (1962).

C.R. Berry and E.L. Glaeser, "The Divergence of Human Capital Levels Across Cities," *Papers in Regional Science* 84:3 (2005) 407–444.

S. Breschi and F. Lissoni, "Localized Knowledge Spillovers vs. Innovative Milieux: Knowledge 'Tacitness' Reconsidered," *Papers in Regional Science* 80:3 (2001) 255–273.

Z. Bronstein, "Industry and Smart City," *Dissent* 56:3 (2009) 27–34.

V. Bush, *Science: The Endless Frontier* (Washington, D.C.: United States Government Printing Office, 1945).

R. Capello, "Spatial Spillovers and Regional Growth: A Cognitive Approach," *European Planning Studies* 17:5 (2009) 639–658.

A. Caragliu and P. Nijkamp, "The Impact of Regional Absorptive Capacity on Spatial Knowledge Spillovers," *Applied Economics* Forthcoming, <www.tandfonline.com/doi/abs/10.1080/00036846.2010.539549> Accessed July 12, 2011.

A. Coe, G. Paquet, and J. Roy, "E-Governance and Smart Communities: A Social Learning Challenge," *Social Science Computer Review* 19:1 (2001).

W. Cohen and D. Levinthal, "Absorptive Capacity: A New Perspective on Learning and Innovation," *Administrative Science Quarterly* 35:1 (1990) 80–93.

D.R. Davis and D.E. Weinstein, "Market Access, Economic Geography, and Comparative Advantage: An Empirical Test," *Journal of International Economics* 59:1 (2003) 128–152.

C. Del Bo and M. Florio, "Infrastructure and Growth in the European Union: An Empirical Analysis at the Regional Level in a Spatial Framework," *Departmental Working Papers 2008-37* (Milan: University of Milan, Department of Economics, 2008), 1–23.

R.L. Florida, *The Rise Of The Creative Class and How It's Transforming Work, Leisure, Community and Everyday Life* (New York: Basic Books, 2002).

R.L. Florida, "Class and Well-Being" (2009), <http://www.creativeclass.com/creative_class/2009/03/17/class-and-well-being/> Accessed March 17, 2009.

S. Fu, "Smart Café Cities: Testing Human Capital Externalities in the Boston Metropolitan Area," *Journal of Urban Economics* 61:1 (2007) 87–111.

E.L. Glaeser, "A Review of Richard Florida's *The Rise Of The Creative Class*," *Regional Science and Urban Economic* 35:5 (2005) 593–596.

E.L. Glaeser and C.R. Berry, "Why Are Smart Places Getting Smarter?" *Taubman Center Policy Brief 2006-2* (Cambridge, MA: John F. Kennedy School of Government, 2006).

S. Graham and S. Marvin, *Telecommunications and the City: Electronic Spaces, Urban Place* (London: Routledge, 1996).

G.H. Hanson, "Market Potential, Increasing Returns, and Geographic Concentration," *Journal of International Economics* 67:1 (2005) 303–320.

R.G. Hollands, "Will The Real Smart City Please Stand Up? Intelligent, Progressive, or Entrepreneurial?" *City* 12:3 (2008) 303–320.

N. Komninos, *Intelligent Cities: Innovation, Knowledge Systems and Digital Spaces* (London: Spon Press, 2002).

R.E. Lucas, "On the Mechanics of Economic Development," *Journal of Monetary Economics* 22:1 (1988) 3–42.

N.G. Mankiw, D. Romer, and D.N. Weil, "A Contribution to the Empirics of Economic Growth," *The Quarterly Journal of Economics* 107:2 (1992) 407–437.

H. Mayer, "What Is the Role of the University in Creating a High-Technology Region?," *Journal of Urban Technology* 14:3 (2007) 33–58.

L.M. Mc Allister, H.M. Hall, H.L. Partridge, and G.C. Hallam, "Effecting Social Change in the 'Smart City': The West End Connect Community Project," paper presented at *Social Change in the 21st Century* (Brisbane, October 28, 2005).

P. Nijkamp, "E Pluribus Unum," *Region Direct* 2:2 (2010) 56–65.

OECD – EUROSTAT, *Oslo Manual* (Paris: Organization for Economic Cooperation and Development, Statistical Office of the European Communities, 2005).

H.L. Partridge, "Developing a Human Perspective to the Digital Divide in the 'Smart City,'" paper presented at the *Australian Library and Information Association Biennial Conference* (Gold Coast, Queensland, September 21-24, 2004).

S. Poelhekke, "Do Amenities and Diversity Encourage City Growth? A Link Through Skilled Labor," *Economics Working Papers ECO2006/10* (2006).

J.E. Rauch, "Productivity Gains from Geographic Concentration of Human Capital: Evidence from the Cities," *Journal of Urban Economics* 34:3 (1993) 380–400.

S.J. Redding and D.M. Sturm, "The Costs of Remoteness: Evidence from German Division and Reunification," *The American Economic Review* 98:5 (2008) 1766–1797.

L-H. Roller and L. Waverman, "Telecommunication Infrastructure and Economic Development: A Simultaneous Approach," *American Economic Review* 91:4 (2001).

J.M. Shapiro, "Smart Cities: Quality Of Life, Productivity, and the Growth Effects of Human Capital," *The Review of Economics and Statistics* 88:2 (2008) 324–335.

Southampton City Council, *Southampton On-Line* (2006) <http://www.southampton.gov.uk/thecouncil/thecouncil/you-and-council/smartcities/> Accessed March 13, 2009.

The Science Museum, *Urban Development* (2004) <http://www.makingthemodernworld.org.uk/learning_modules/geography/04.TU.01/?section=2> Accessed April 3, 2009.

United Nations, *World Urbanization Prospects: The 2009 revision* (2009) <http://esa.un.org/unpd/wup/index.htm> Accessed February 15, 2011.

UNESCO. *International Standardization of Educational Statistics* (2006) <www.uis.unesco.org/Library/Documents/isced97-en.pdf>

Appendix: Urban Audit Codes and City Names

Urban Audit Code	City Name
at001c	Wien
at002c	Graz
at003c	Linz
be001c	Bruxelles
be002c	Antwerpen
be003c	Gent
be004c	Charleroi
be005c	Liège
be006c	Brugge
bg001c	Sofia
bg002c	Plovdiv
bg003c	Varna
bg004c	Burgas
bg005c	Pleven
bg006c	Ruse
bg007c	Vidin
ch001c	Zürich
ch002c	Genève
ch004c	Bern
ch005c	Lausanne
cy001c	Lefkosia
cz001c	Praha
cz002c	Brno
cz003c	Ostrava
cz004c	Plzen
cz005c	Usti nad Labem
de001c	Berlin
de002c	Hamburg
de003c	München
de004c	Köln
de005c	Frankfurt am Main
de006c	Essen
de008c	Leipzig
de009c	Dresden
de010c	Dortmund
de011c	Düsseldorf
de012c	Bremen
de013c	Hannover
de014c	Nürnberg
de015c	Bochum
de016c	Wuppertal
de017c	Bielefeld
de018c	Halle an der Saale
de019c	Magdeburg
de020c	Wiesbaden
de021c	Göttingen
de022c	Mülheim a.d.Ruhr
de023c	Moers
de025c	Darmstadt
de026c	Trier
de027c	Freiburg im Breisgau
de028c	Regensburg
de029c	Frankfurt (Oder)
de030c	Weimar

Continued

Urban Audit Code	City Name
de031c	Schwerin
de032c	Erfurt
de033c	Augsburg
de034c	Bonn
de035c	Karlsruhe
de036c	Mönchengladbach
de037c	Mainz
dk001c	Copenhagen
dk002c	Aarhus
dk003c	Odense
dk004c	Aalborg
ee001c	Tallinn
ee002c	Tartu
es001c	Madrid
es002c	Barcelona
es003c	Valencia
es004c	Sevilla
es005c	Zaragoza
es006c	Málaga
es007c	Murcia
es008c	Las Palmas
es009c	Valladolid
es010c	Palma di Mallorca
es011c	Santiago de Compostela
es012c	Vitoria/Gasteiz
es013c	Oviedo
es014c	Pamplona/Iruña
es015c	Santander
es016c	Toledo
es017c	Badajoz
es018c	Logroño
fi001c	Helsinki
fi002c	Tampere
fi003c	Turku
fi004c	Oulu
fr001c	Paris
fr003c	Lyon
fr004c	Toulouse
fr006c	Strasbourg
fr007c	Bordeaux
fr008c	Nantes
fr009c	Lille
fr010c	Montpellier
fr011c	Saint-Etienne
fr012c	Le Havre
fr013c	Rennes
fr014c	Amiens
fr015c	Rouen
fr016c	Nancy
fr017c	Metz
fr018c	Reims
fr019c	Orléans
fr020c	Dijon
fr021c	Poitiers

(Continued) *(Continued)*

Continued

Urban Audit Code	City Name
fr022c	Clermont-Ferrand
fr023c	Caen
fr024c	Limoges
fr025c	Besançon
fr026c	Grenoble
fr027c	Ajaccio
fr028c	Saint Denis
fr029c	Pointe-a-Pitre
fr030c	Fort-de-France
fr031c	Cayenne
fr032c	Toulon
fr035c	Tours
fr202c	Aix-en-Provence
fr203c	Marseille
fr205c	Nice
fr207c	Lens - Liévin
gr001c	Athina
gr002c	Thessaloniki
gr003c	Patra
gr004c	Iraklio
gr005c	Larissa
gr006c	Volos
gr007c	Ioannina
gr008c	Kavala
gr009c	Kalamata
hu001c	Budapest
hu002c	Miskolc
hu003c	Nyiregyhaza
hu004c	Pecs
ie001c	Dublin
ie002c	Cork
ie003c	Limerick
ie004c	Galway
it001c	Roma
it002c	Milano
it003c	Napoli
it004c	Torino
it005c	Palermo
it006c	Genova
it007c	Firenze
it008c	Bari
it009c	Bologna
it010c	Catania
it011c	Venezia
it012c	Verona
it013c	Cremona
it014c	Trento
it015c	Trieste
it016c	Perugia
it017c	Ancona
it018c	l'Aquila
it019c	Pescara
it020c	Campobasso
it021c	Caserta

(Continued)

Continued

Urban Audit Code	City Name
it022c	Taranto
it023c	Potenza
it024c	Catanzaro
it025c	Reggio di Calabria
it026c	Sassari
it027c	Cagliari
lt001c	Vilnius
lt002c	Kaunas
lt003c	Panevezys
lu001c	Luxembourg
lv001c	Riga
lv002c	Liepaja
mt001c	Valletta
nl001c	s' Gravenhage
nl002c	Amsterdam
nl003c	Rotterdam
nl004c	Utrecht
nl005c	Eindhoven
nl006c	Tilburg
nl007c	Groningen
nl008c	Enschede
nl009c	Arnhem
nl010c	Heerlen
pl001c	Warszawa
pl002c	Lodz
pl003c	Krakow
pl004c	Wroclaw
pl005c	Poznan
pl006c	Gdansk
pl007c	Szczecin
pl008c	Bydgoszcz
pl009c	Lublin
pl010c	Katowice
pl011c	Bialystok
pl012c	Kielce
pl013c	Torun
pl014c	Olsztyn
pl015c	Rzeszow
pl016c	Opole
pl017c	Gorzow Wielkopolski
pl018c	Zielona Gora
pl019c	Jelenia Gora
pl020c	Nowy Sacz
pl021c	Suwalki
pl022c	Konin
pl023c	Zory
pt001c	Lisboa
pt002c	Oporto
pt003c	Braga
pt004c	Funchal
pt005c	Coimbra
pt006c	Setubal
pt007c	Ponto Delgada
pt008c	Aveiro

(Continued)

Continued

Urban Audit Code	City Name
ro001c	Bucuresti
ro002c	Cluj-Napoca
ro003c	Timisoara
ro004c	Craiova
ro005c	Braila
ro006c	Oradea
ro007c	Bacau
ro008c	Arad
ro009c	Sibiu
ro010c	Targu Mures
ro011c	Piatra Neamt
ro012c	Calarasi
ro013c	Giurgiu
ro014c	Alba Iulia
se001c	Stockholm
se002c	Göteborg
se003c	Malmö
se004c	Jönköping
se005c	Umeå
si001c	Ljubljana
si002c	Maribor
sk001c	Bratislava
sk002c	Kosice
sk003c	Banska Bystrica

(*Continued*)

Continued

Urban Audit Code	City Name
sk004c	Nitra
uk001c	London
uk002c	Birmingham
uk003c	Leeds
uk004c	Glasgow
uk005c	Bradford
uk006c	Liverpool
uk007c	Edinburgh
uk008c	Manchester
uk009c	Cardiff
uk010c	Sheffield
uk011c	Bristol
uk012c	Belfast
uk013c	Newcastle upon Tyne
uk014c	Leicester
uk015c	Derry
uk016c	Aberdeen
uk017c	Cambridge
uk018c	Exeter
uk019c	Lincoln
uk020c	Gravesham
uk021c	Stevenage
uk022c	Wrexham
uk023c	Portsmouth
uk024c	Worcester

SCRAN: The Network

Peter Cruickshank

ABSTRACT *This paper outlines the relationship between the Smart Cities (inter)Regional Academic Network (SCRAN) and the triple-helix model of knowledge production, a model encompassing industry, the university, and the government. The "step-wise" logic of SCRAN's triple helix for the SmartCities venture is then set out. This draws attention to the networking of the intellectual capital underpinning SCRAN's knowledge base and learning platform. From here the paper goes on to set out how SCRAN's wiki is being used to match the intellectual capital and wealth creation of the SmartCities' triple helix with the e-government services developing under the North Sea's regional innovation system.*

Introduction

The concept of the "smart city" has been introduced as a strategic device to encompass modern urban production factors in a common framework. As such it serves to highlight two emerging trends: the growing importance of information and communication technologies (ICTs) in the development of cities and the growing use of social and environmental capital as measures of the competitiveness of cities (Deakin, 2010; Caragliu et al., 2009). These assets—social and environmental capital—distinguish smart cities from their more technology-laden counterparts, drawing a clear line between their ICTs and what otherwise goes under the name of either digital or intelligent cities.

To highlight the significance of these assets, this paper draws attention to the triple-helix model of knowledge production and to the wiki assembled to support the development of the Smart Cities (inter) Regional Academic Network (SCRAN) as a community of practice (CoP). It draws particular attention to the university-industry-government collaborations (triple helix) underlying the Web 2.0 service-orientated architecture of this knowledge infrastructure and the deployment of such technologies as an enterprise allowing communities to learn about how to standardize e-government (eGov) services as transformative business-to-citizen applications. This serves to highlight the critical role such business-to-citizen applications play in making it possible for cities to be smart in reaching beyond the transactional logic of service provision and grasping the potential that regional innovation systems have to democratize the ongoing customization of e-government.[1]

In this context, CoPs cover a number of situated practices, with characteristics including shared ways of "doing things together," "using specific tools and other artifacts" (Wenger, 1998). Recently, the "learning-by-doing" and "action-based" logic of this model has been extended to cover virtual organizations and online interaction (Amin and Roberts, 2008). CoPs defined as "virtual organizations" are commonly referred to as "Type 2" communities and draw upon lessons learned from the practical experiences of knowledge-based networks: that is, from the assembly and subsequent deployment of virtual organizations that are created to share the best practices of developing their infrastructures. The growing significance of CoPs and what they contribute to the competitiveness of cities has recently been highlighted in the work published on the IntelCities CoP (Deakin, 2009). This paper draws on the lessons learned from this CoP and transfers the best practices of this venture to the (virtual) organization known as SCRAN.

After reflecting on the communication needs and technical requirements of this venture, the paper goes on to configure SCRAN's triple helix and set out the "step-wise" logic of the organization's knowledge base and learning platform. From here attention turns towards the networking of the triple helix and the wiki assembled to support the development of SCRAN as a community of practice. Here attention is drawn to the university-industry-government collaborations (triple helix) underlying the Web 2.0 service-orientated architecture of this knowledge infrastructure and the deployment of such technologies as an enterprise for organizations to learn about how this CoP works to standardize the transformation of e-government services. This is important to cities because standardized e-government services can transform business-citizen applications and allow them to be "smart" by integrating the business sector into the North Sea regional innovation system.

Academic Networking of the SmartCities Venture

Figure 1 illustrates the academic network underpinning the SmartCities venture known as SCRAN. It identifies the network of academic institutions, their city partners, and the specific roles they play within SCRAN. As can be seen, for Edinburgh Napier University the main object of attention is methodology and for Mechelen (MEMORI) the object of the exercise is to partner with Kortrijk in their customization of e-government services. Each academic institution involved in the SmartCities venture, along with its respective industrial and government partner, is seen as contributing to the knowledge base that is necessary for developing e-government services.

SCRAN as a Three-Way Partnership

While the aforesaid draws attention to academic institutions and their city partners, it is the three-way partnership among universities, industry, and government that captures the science and technology around which the "triple helix" turns. This offers an image of the triple helix that SCRAN proposes to develop as a three-way partnership that delivers on one aspect of the EC-funded SmartCities project that supports the innovative and creative use of ICTs.

From here the organizational means needed for universities and their industrial counterparts to use ICTs in the development of e-government (eGov) services can be explored in terms of the capabilities of the partners. The partners construct a methodology capable of supporting the development of eGov services and

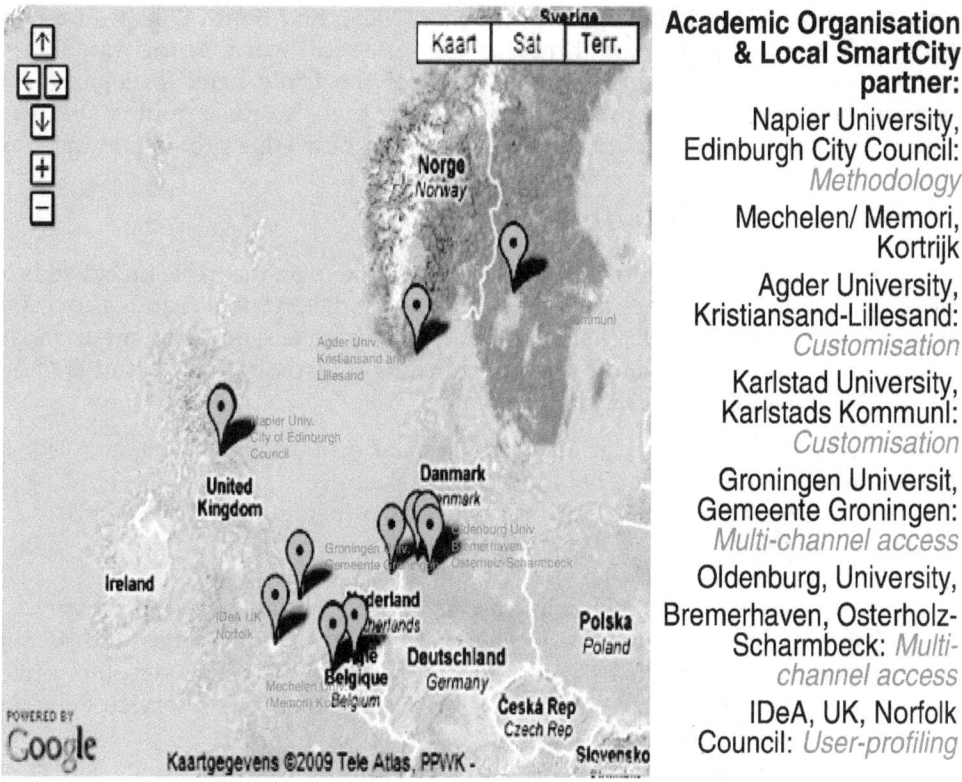

Figure 1. Academic organization of SmartCities partner(s)

building the capacity to co-design them in a way that allows the user-profiles of this constituency to be mainstreamed across the North Sea region.

The Triple Helix

As the main exponents of the triple helix, Etzkowitz and Leydesdorff (2003; 2008) offer a particularly insightful critique of so-called "mode 2" accounts of innovation, i.e., the kind of innovation that is problem-focused and interdisciplinary. They limit their particular representation of the model to those institutional relations surrounding university, industry and government involvement in the knowledge economy of regional systems. Here attention focuses on the production of knowledge by universities and industry as an index of the intellectual capital tied up in the artifacts of innovations patented and licensed in line with the standards laid down by government to regulate such developments.

As critically insightful as these studies are, they are limited to output-related examinations of knowledge production and tend to ignore the infrastructure underlying the institutional relations supporting the involvement of universities, industry, and government in this process. Institutionally-based studies of this type are limited and as a result, little is known about either the ICTs that underlie the triple helix or the electronically-enhanced services upon which the model's understanding of knowledge production rests. Understandably, the absence of such studies has led to criticism about the usefulness of the triple helix as a model of knowledge production and its value as a regional innovation system. Jensen and Tragardh (2004), Jauhiainen and Suorsa (2008), and Smith (2007) raise concerns about the triple helix and question the practical worth of the model. The apparent reluctance of the main exponents of the triple helix to engage in a debate about the model's practical worth also serves to raise doubts about its capacity to adequately account for the process of knowledge production in cities.

SCRAN's Take on the Triple Helix

To overcome these limitations, it is clear SCRAN's take on the triple helix needs to develop practical guidelines on how to use the model and this requires covering the three strands of the helix, i.e. universities, industry, and government. In methodological terms, the challenge this poses means SCRAN has to account for how the triple helix of SmartCities can organize:

- the production of knowledge internally (i.e., as a smart city)
- externally as part of a regional innovation system
- as a way of systematically "turning innovation inside out" and doing this by representing the:
  - triple helix of smart cities
  - organization of this as the social capital underlying the knowledge base
  - collaboration needed for the intellectual capital of universities and wealth creation of industry to be smart in constructing the advantage this offers cities to learn how their communities can meet their eGov service development commitments
  - consensus-building needed for this reinvention of cities to be smart in supporting the development of "trans-national" standards regulating the development of eGov services
  - practical application of such standards in building the capacity required to be "post-transactional," which means that businesses and citizens are able to participate in the development of eGov services.

The unique nature of this academic network rests on understanding that triple-helix models are not just about offering theoretically-informed research and technical development opportunities, but a methodology capable of accounting for the social capital of the knowledge base available for communities to learn about how cities can be(come) smart. This is because with SCRAN, research and technical development are not the network's common denominators, as its particular terms of reference lie elsewhere—with the academic contribution the network makes to the intellectual capital of the SmartCities venture. That contribution is the social capital that the academic network constructs (Halpern, 2005) by providing the knowledge base of this learning community (Deakin and Allwinkle, 2005, Riemer and Stefan, 2008).

SCRAN's particular task is to discover how the intellectual capital of the knowledge base underlying this learning community is able to become a platform that supports the wealth creation of industry while being regulated by government through electronically enhanced services.

Configuring the SmartCities Triple Helix

Figure 2 sets out SCRAN's attempt to meet the methodological challenges such a process of knowledge production raises and offers an initial representation of the

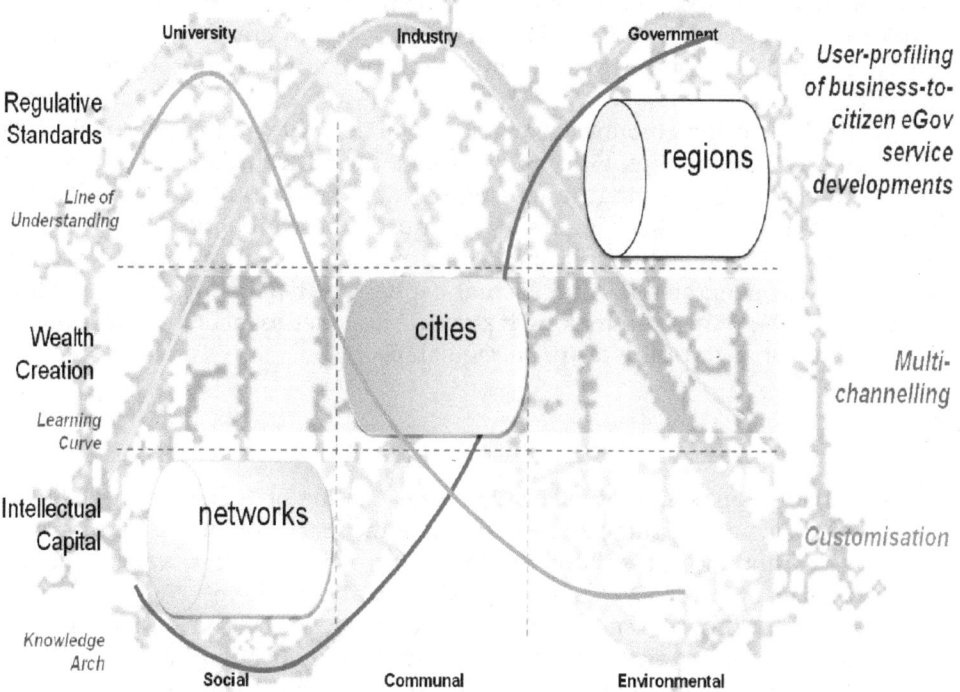

Figure 2. The triple helix of SmartCities

Notes: [1]Unlike most triple helix studies that rest upon the knowledge economy of information society, this representation is not set in the fundamental, or strategic research ('blue-sky', or 'applied') domain of either a pre-dominantly science and technology, or entrepreneurial-led University, but the intellectual capital which is generated from their 'third mission' outreach into social networks as the knowledge base of wealth creation.

[2]The intellectual capital embedded in these social networks offers the technological basis to begin understanding how industry organize communities so it becomes possible for them to learn about how they can manage the knowledge invested in this process of wealth creation.

[3]The intellectual capital of this wealth creation in turn calls for government involvement in setting the standards for eGov service developments to regulate this process.

[4]This wealth of intellect in turn offers the depth of academic understanding, social learning and communal knowledge needed for the development of eGov services to regulate all of this a part of a regional innovation system.

[5]This is why the focus of this triple helix is on the knowledge base of those learning platforms supporting cities, rather than understanding the standards of regulation governing regional innovation systems. That knowledge and learning which takes place here by way of cities and through the industry of their wealth creation. The industry of their wealth creation which is seen to be smart for the reason it is these communities that offer the means (intellectual capital of socially-embedded networks and industry of wealth creation) to understand the nature of the developments in question.

[6]In many respects this (re)modeling of the triple helix does what Jensen and Tragardh (2004), Jauhiainen and Suorsa (2008) and Smith (2007) ask of it.

triple helix that the SmartCities Project advances for such purposes. In semantic terms, the three institutional dimensions of universities, industry, and government are represented as the intellectual capital, wealth creation, and regulation of eGov service developments and as that process of knowledge production that is part of the North Sea's regional innovation system. Set out as an actor-network matrix of such institutional relations, it is universities, industry, and government that make up the columns of the matrix and their respective contributions to the generation of intellectual capital, wealth creation, and regulative standards of the developments that make up the knowledge production of the left hand row.

While the specific guidance available from Etzkowitz and Leydesdorff (2000) is particularly limited here, Figure 2 does take a lead from Leydesdorff's (2006) and Etzkowitz's (2008) configurations of the triple helix and "geometries" of the model's reflexive qualities. Figure 2 configures these qualities as a three-by-three matrix that shows the building blocks of a social network having a knowledge base that generates the intellectual capital needed for the wealth created by industry to be "smart" in making it possible for cities to meet the government's requirement for such processes to be regulated.

The Step-Wise Logic

This first institutional step into a formal representation of SCRAN's triple helix is given content by means of the analytical spaces the matrix opens up for the Smart-Cities venture and the opportunity this in turn provides the three-way partnership to become part of the North Sea's regional innovation system.

This networking of SmartCities as a regional innovation system, in turn, relates the universities engaged in the generation of intellectual capital, the industries involved in the creation of wealth and the government regulating the standards of the service development (i.e., the generation of wealth from the development of eGov services) back to those actors associating with one another as a learning community. Step two of Figure 2 captures this in terms of the wealth created by this process of knowledge production, and what learning this community contributes is represented in the right-hand column of the matrix. This is shown in terms of the advantage that smart cities build as a platform of wealth creation regulated by the development of eGov services. All of this is then captured as step three and is represented in the far right-hand column of Figure 2. This is shown in terms of what the wealth of knowledge produced contributes to the development of eGov services as part of a regional innovation system.

Inverting the Normal Representation

Revealing how the triple-helix of the SmartCities venture can be organized to be constructive is, however, not simple. This is because proving that it needs to be socially-inclusive, equitable, and justly participative, requires the academic network to accept the value of the requirement to first "invert" the normal representation of the model's institutional relations. For without "turning things up-side down," it is not possible for the intellectual capital of universities to be deployed in bottoming-out the social networks that make up the knowledge base of the learning communities that industry organizes as the "intellectual wealth" of smart cities and the standards by which the development of electronically-enhanced services by government are regulated across the region.

Figure 3 offers SCRAN's attempt to do just this by presenting a second-order configuration of the triple helix for SmartCities. For this configuration shows the university as being responsible for building the capacity of the enterprise

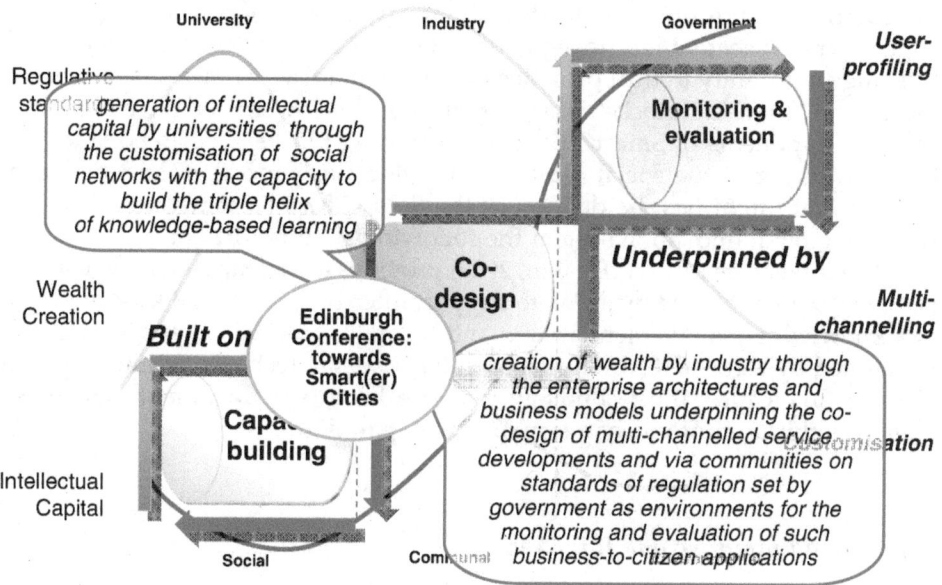

Figure 3. The triple helix of SmartCities

architecture and business models to act as a platform for cities to be smart in co-designing the development of eGov services with customized, multi-channeled access, targeting specific user-profiles as components of the North Sea's regional innovation system.

Represented in this way, it is possible to be specific about the institutional duties and responsibilities of SCRAN's triple helix. For as Figure 3 shows, while the work packaged together under the titles of: customization, co-design, and user-profiling, provides the backdrop to SCRAN, it is not proposed that SmartCities should cover all of these as components of the North Sea's regional innovation system. Rather it suggests SCRAN should use the triple-helix model as a means to cut across them, concentrating the efforts of the network's knowledge base on learning about building the capacity needed for cities to be "smart" in supporting the co-design, monitoring, and evaluation requirements of eGov service development programs. That capacity-building is central to the generation of the intellectual capital of social networks.

Organized in this way, it is possible to see the geometry of the "knowledge-arch" and "learning curve" that underlies SCRAN's take on the triple helix. What this also serves to illustrate is the academic network's particular take on such an institutionalization of the model. In particular, the triple helix builds off the social network of a given knowledge base and allows universities to take the lead in generating the wealth of industry They do this through enterprise architectures and business models that are particularly important to SCRAN because they not only offer a platform for the associated capital of the communities to learn about what the customization, co-design, and multi-channeling of services means, but also because they offer a way to monitor and evaluate the implementation of eGov developments as part of a regional innovation system.

Of course, for universities to be part of something more than an informal social network means the academic content of the capital associated with any such learning community demands a pedagogy capable of constructing a knowledge of what is needed for the regulation of the wealth created. The content of this learning community in turn provides the platform for what might best be termed the critical "building-blocks" of smart cities and eGov service development. As critical components of SmartCities, these building blocks need to be linked. It is the networking of the social capital underlying this process of knowledge production that might best be defined as the SmartCities learning community and whose regional innovation system the following shall report on.

The IntelCities project (Deakin, 2009) provides an example of how just such a pedagogy can deployed by a CoP to support inter-organizational learning by way of a knowledge-management system and through a digital library. This CoP can be defined by three features: a shared enterprise, the technology, and online services. In IntelCities, the technology took the form of a document management system within the context of a semantic web paradigm.

The Shared Enterprise and Joint Venture

The enterprise represented by SCRAN is based on a collaboration and partnership that is constructed through consensus-building. The communication that is essential to the collaboration is facilitated by the platforms that connect the networked communities and allow them to share knowledge about both wealth creation and governance opportunities. Sometimes the democratic qualities of these spaces are overlooked by those attending to only the community-building and environmental components of these networks. However, the democratic aspects are apparent when it is recognized that the body of knowledge circulated through the networks includes practices that are both representative and participative.

The three dimensions of the venture are summarized in Figure 4, which illustrates that networking has been used as the means by which to collaborate and build consensus (primarily by SCRAN) regarding service developments. This, in turn, has built the capacity to serve the co-design and monitoring and evalu-

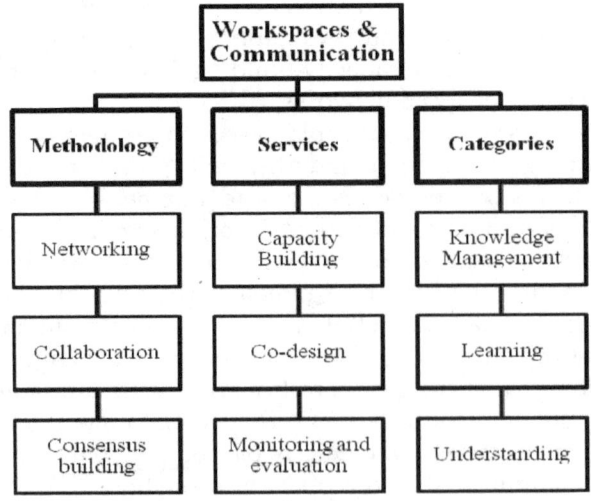

Figure 4. The three dimensions of workplace and communication

ation needs of their respective knowledge management, learning, and understanding requirements.

It is possible to explore the service development set out in Figure 4 further. First, the heading of capacity building focuses attention on the technical issues and, in particular, on those supporting the partnership's enterprise architecture and business modeling. From here attention turns to the co-design of the customized and multi-channeled use of the eGov services. Finally, in terms of the monitoring and evaluation, questions of particular relevance surfacing here relate to the degree to which the development of eGov services raises standards of provision by:

- improving the quality of service provision through an enhanced customer experience
- better matching customer needs with the required services
- widening access to the services (via multi-channel access) and being socially inclusive in deciding where the services are directed
- being more efficient (cost-effective) and democratically accountable in delivering the services relative to other modes of provision.

To meet these standards four web-service developments are required:

- information provision
- collaboration and consensus building
- knowledge management
- learning and (shared) understanding.

The SCRAN Wiki

While a variety of collaborative platforms are available, consensus was reached regarding the need for SCRAN to put information systems in place that are simple, lightweight, and robust. Those systems also had to be agile enough to meet the growing requirements of the venture's learning community. The first requirement was for a content management system (CMS) and that was provided by the content-management platform Drupal.[2]

The communications needs and tools used by SmartCities are summarized in Figure 5. Fortunately, it is now possible to offer the academic organizations and local SmartCities partners all of these web-services by way of a wiki. In this regard, Mediawiki[3] was selected by SCRAN for its flexibility in supporting the network's knowledge management and learning requirements. This software allows users to freely create and edit web page content using any web browser. Wikis also support hyperlinks and have a simple text syntax for creating new pages and cross-links between internal documents. Because wikis allow users to create and edit any page on a web site, they are a way for civil society to democratize the use of the Internet.

Evolution of the Knowledge Base

The wiki was initially designed to support communication between SCRAN and other SmartCities partners. This challenge has been met by developing a glossary to help with the terminology of eGov service developments and a questioning framework, supported by a set of research briefs. (See Figure 6.)

Requirement	Tools Used
1. Information:	
Public web-site	Drupal
News and events	Epractice.eu
2. Collaboration & consensus building:	
Transient messages	Email, mailing list
Record of meetings	Drupal (login required)
Activity planning	Private Mediawiki pages
Discussions	Email
Formal decisions	(Face to face at project meetings)
3. Knowledge management	
Glossary	Mediawiki pages, cross linked to work package and expertise
Digital library	Documents stored on Mediawiki or Drupal
Search engine	Public pages: Drupal and Google search Private pages: Mediawiki search, use of categories, automatic cross-linking
4. Learning and understanding	
Good practice	Private Mediawiki pages
Case studies	Private Mediawiki pages
Use cases	Private Mediawiki pages + supporting documents

Figure 5. Choice of technology to support the needs of SmartCities

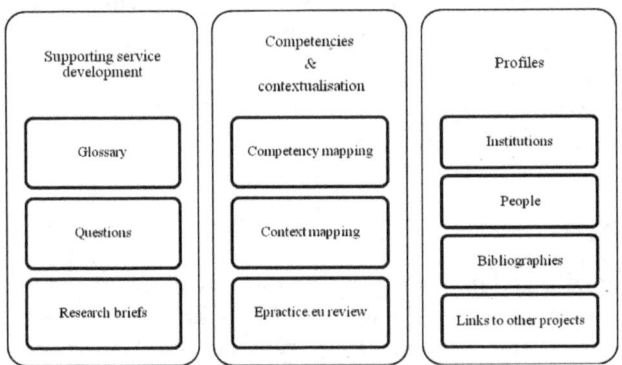

Figure 6. Initial architecture of the SmartCities wiki

This architecture is also reflected in the relatively simple initial home page illustrated in Figure 7. From the start, the need to be disciplined in the use of categories and structured templates has been recognized. The first task carried out was a competence mapping of the SCRAN partners, providing a direct link between them and the work that contextualizes the developments.

Next, a context-mapping exercise was performed to gain an insight into the issues underlying the evolution of eGov services for each municipal partner, thus identifying the effects of eGov service developments on governments. Finally, alternative sources of knowledge management and learning were reviewed by examining cases studies stored on the database that is maintained by <epractice.eu>. This is a portal for practitioners working in e-government and promoted by the EC as a benchmark of current knowledge and understanding.[4]

As the project has progressed, the use of the wiki has evolved. Merely looking at the home page at the start of 2010 (See Figure 8.) shows how content of the wiki has become richer as the project has progressed and the practitioners have become engaged in the process.

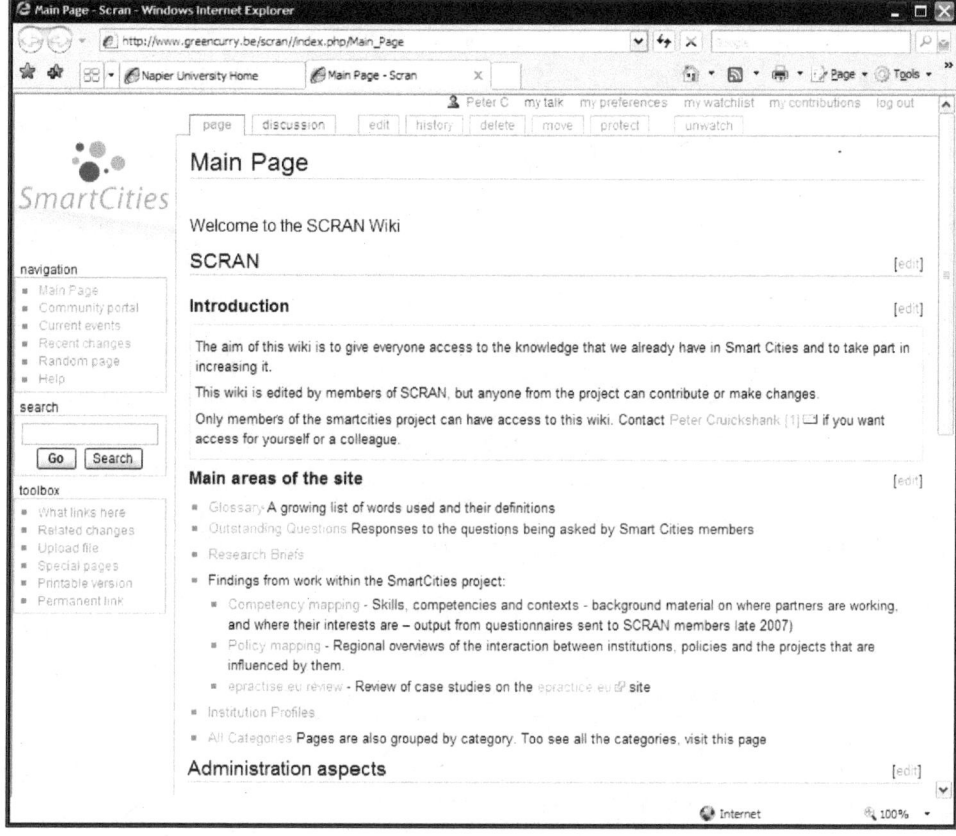

Figure 7. The initial web page of SCRAN's wiki

Case Study Review

<Epractice.eu> is a major resource and dissemination tool for European projects. As an exercise, SCRAN explored and assessed the data it holds on cases to highlight good practices relevant to the development of eGov services in the North Sea Region.

The exercise was designed to identify case studies submitted by <epractice.eu>. This found 30 potentially relevant cases that were reviewed for quality and relevance to the SmartCities venture, as a result of which the data set was pared down to 16. Out of the 16, only one of them referenced the triple-helix model of eGov service developments.[5]

Figure 9 shows the frequency of occurrence of keywords in the investigated cases. It is evident the common denominators with the SmartCities venture rest with their focus on policy, e-Gov services, multi-channel access, user-centric services, and interoperable infrastructure technologies. Perhaps more significant is the lack of any reference to the enterprise architecture and business model of an open system, along with any notion of what it means to customize eGov services.[6] For while the case studies go some way to highlight the need for core infrastructure developments (i.e., secure access and the security of personal data), it is evident they offer little by way of critical insight into the underlying methodology of the inclusive policy agenda they flag up for the multi-channeling and user-profiling services they draw attention to.

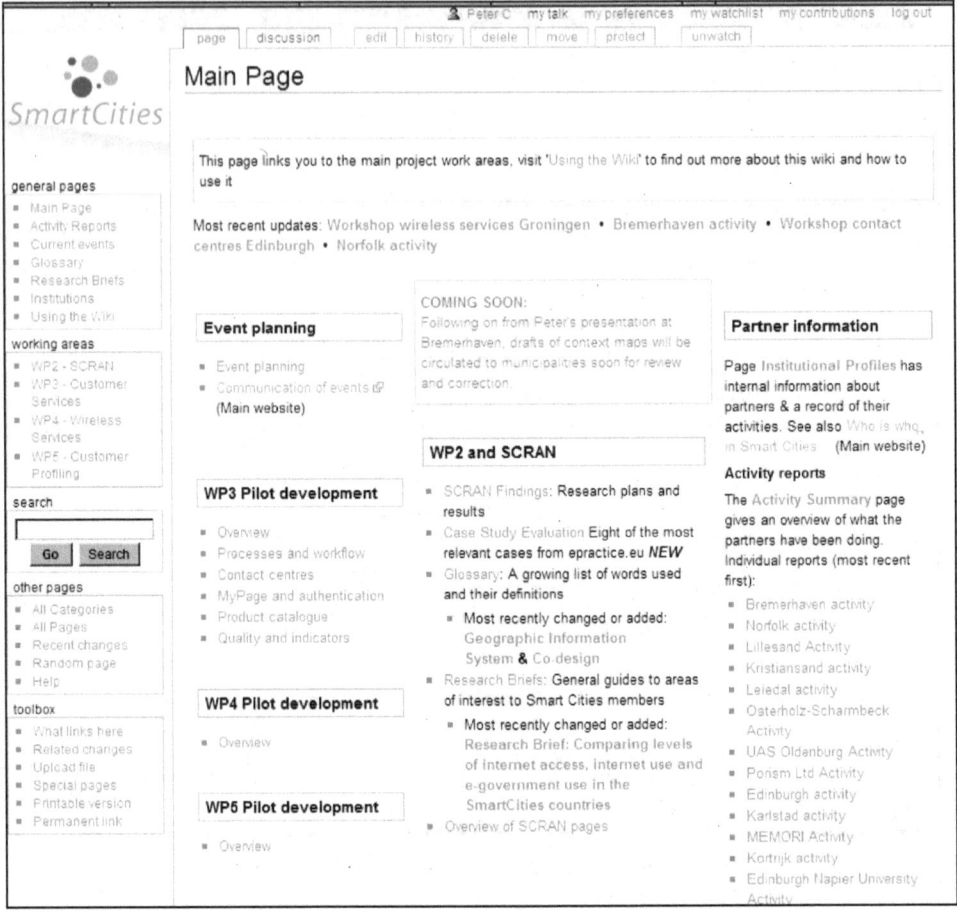

Figure 8. The wiki home page after one year

This lack of critical insight is significant insofar as it raises particular questions about civil society's trust in the ability of electronically-enhanced services to be secure enough for them do anything but store data and transfer information. That lack of trust inhibits the use of the types of transactions that SmartCities proposed to customize and offer as eGov services. These transactions are particularly important because they provide a platform for the type of consultations and deliberations that SmartCities seek to develop.

It is evident that to do this an enterprise architecture and business model should be the basis for the customization of eGov services. That customization can be achieved through the support of trans-national pilots that will allow multi-channel access and user-profiling of business-to-citizen applications that can emerge as key components of regional innovation systems.

Commissioning of Work

SCRAN also oversees a fund available to meet the cost of commissioning research and consultancy by the business community. The fund is designed to take the triple-helix model full circle and commission work from university and industry sectors capable

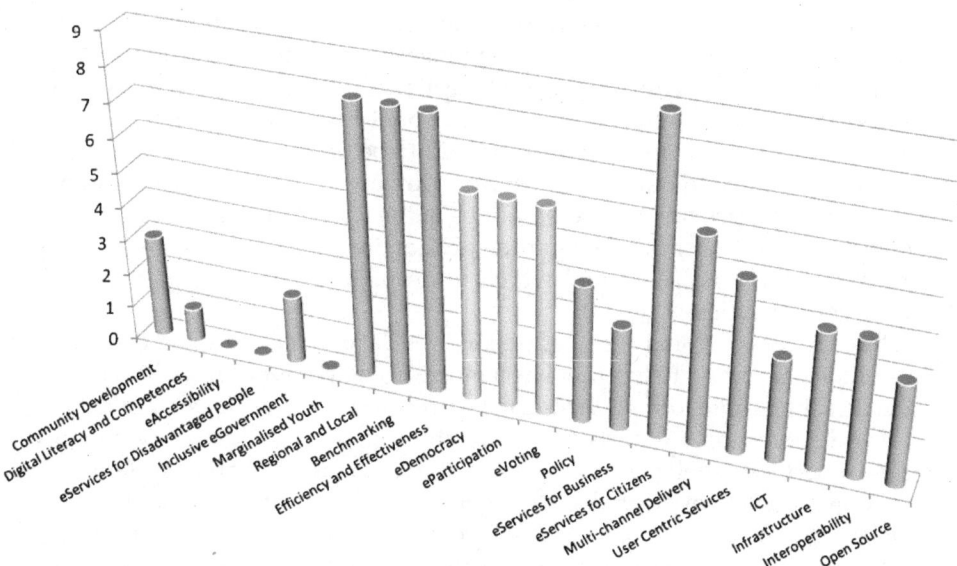

Figure 9. Frequency of self-labeled categories used in cases listed on <epractice.eu>

of consulting on the use of ICTs as a means of networking social capital. The work commissioned aligns with the enterprise architecture and business modeling needs of the capacity building, co-design, and evaluation and monitoring requirements underlying the SmartCities venture. This in turn allows the work commissioned to:

- operationalize a triple-helix model of eGov service developments
- draw upon this knowledge base as a platform to build eGov services
- use the collective memory of this learning community as a means to instill a sense of identity that can embody the wisdom attached to three-way partnerships of this kind
- deploy that wisdom as part of a step change in eGov service developments and use this as a means to mainstream them as part of the North Sea's regional innovation system.

Conclusions

This paper has focused on the SCRAN's model of the triple helix for the SmartCities venture and drawn attention to the communication needs and the organizational and technical requirements of the network that facilitates the transfer of knowledge about eGov programs among cities.

In meeting this aim, the paper has reported on the three-way partnership working in the SmartCities venture, the methodology underlying the development of SCRAN as a network, the web-services supporting the organization's efforts, the commissioning of work from the business sector, and the governance of this particular development process. It has gone on to configure SCRAN's triple helix and set out the "step-wise" logic of the organization's knowledge base and learning platform. From here attention has turned towards the networking of the triple helix by way of SCRAN's Wiki and through the learning community supporting the SmartCities venture.

These developments are seen to be significant because under this representation of the triple helix, university engagement is no longer a top-down exercise in either the generation of intellectual capital or the creation of wealth, but a bottom-up exercise in building the social capital regulating the development of eGov services. Such involvement can be said to be bottomed-out on the networking of social capital and out with the normal domain of the triple helix. This in turn tends to undercut previous representations of the triple helix, so much so that here the object of the exercise is no longer the production of a knowledge economy, but the creation of the social capital which underpins the knowledge base of their learning communities.

Here the social capital is embedded in Web 2.0 technologies and their learning community's ambition to use them as a means to work smarter not harder. This in turn makes it possible for knowledge to be produced with sufficient critical insight to over-ride economic interests and grant civil society sufficient power to govern over eGov service developments as part of the regional innovation system it is part of. Making all of this explicit also allows SCRAN to improve the quality of service provision by way of such business-to-citizen applications and through a process of customization available over the web via multi-channel access and in line with the user-profiles governing developments of this type.

All this does nothing less than operationalize SCRAN's triple-helix model by allowing the network to use the capacities of the communities that it creates as the platform by which to learn about the development of eGov services. This also serves to standardize the transformation of e-Government as a triple-helix of Web-2.0-based knowledge infrastructures, architectures, and enterprises that, in turn, allow organizations to learn about the critical role which business-to-citizen applications play in making it possible for cities to become smart in reaching beyond the transactional logic of service provision and grasping the potential their regional innovation systems have to democratize this transformation.

This possibility is something that has all too often been missed by those reporting on the democratic transformation of e-Government services currently underway and yet critical in understanding: whether the generation of intellectual capital by universities allows cities to be "smart" in creating wealth and if industry's deployment of such business-to-citizen applications as the democratic means to govern regional innovation systems are developments capable of regulating such exchanges. This offers an image of the triple helix that SCRAN proposes to develop, for it not only goes some way to capture this organization's particular take on the triple helix, but also serves as a means by which this particular CoP can draw attention to the scientific and technological basis of the SmartCities venture.

Notes

1. http://www.northsearegion.eu/ivb/projects/details/&tid=84
2. http://www.drupal.org
3. http://www.mediawiki.org/
4. A secondary motivation is that <epractice.eu> also provides the primary route for Europe-wide dissemination of project activities.
5. The Swedish innovation body INNOVA <http://www.vinnova.se/>
6. Again only one case provides evidence of a service-orientated enterprise architecture for eGov developments and there are no references to any underlying business models.

Bibliography

A. Amin and J. Roberts, "Knowing in Action: Beyond Communities of Practice," *Research Policy* 37:2 (2008) 353–369.

A. Caragliu, C. Del Bo, and P. Nijkamp, "Smart Cities in Europe," *Serie Research Memoranda 0048* (2009), <http://ideas.repec.org/p/dgr/vuarem/2009-48.html> Accessed April 6, 2011.

M. Deakin, "The IntelCities Community of Practice: The eGov Services Model for Socially-Inclusive and Participatory Urban Regeneration Programmes," in C. Riddeck, ed., *Research Strategies for eGovernment Service Adoption* (Hershey: Idea Group Publishing, 2009).

M. Deakin, "SCRAN: The SmartCities (inter) Regional Academic Network Supporting the Development of a Trans-National Comparator for the Standardisation of e-Government Services," in C. Reddick, ed., *Comparative E-government: An Examination of E-Government Across Countries* (Berlin: Springer Press, 2010).

M. Deakin and S. Allwinkle, "The IntelCities eLearning Platform, Knowledge Management System and Digital Library for Semantically Interoperable e-Governance Services," in P. Cunningham, ed., *Innovation and the Knowledge Economy: Issues, Applications, and Case Studies* (Washington, D.C: ISO Press, 2005).

H. Etzkowitz, *The Triple Helix: University-Industry-Government Innovation in Action* (Oxon: Routledge, 2008).

H. Etzkowitz and L. Leydesdorff, "The Dynamics of Innovation: From National Systems and 'Mode 2' to a Triple Helix of University–Industry–Government Relations," *Research Policy* 29 (2000) 109–123.

H. Etzkowitz and L. Leydesdorff, eds., *Universities and the Global Knowledge Economy NIP: A Triple Helix of University-Industry-Government Relations* (London: Continuum International Publishing Group Ltd, 2008).

H. Etzkowitz and L. Leydesdorff, "Can 'the Public' Be Considered as a Fourth Helix in University-Industry-Government Relations? Report of the Fourth Triple Helix Conference," *Science & Public Policy* 30:1 (2003) 55–61.

D. Halpern, *Social Capital* (Bristol: Polity Press, 2005).

J. Jauhiainen and K. Suorsa, "Triple Helix in the Periphery: The Case of Multipolis in Northern Finland," *Cambridge Journal of Regions, Economy, and Society* 1:2 (2008) 285–301.

C. Jensen and B. Tragardh, "Narrating the Triple Helix Concept in 'Weak' Regions: Lessons from Sweden," *International Journal of Technology Management* 27(5) (2004) 513–530.

L. Leydesdorff, *The Knowledge-Based Economy: Modeled, Measured and Simulated* (Florida: Universal Publishers, 2006).

K. Riemer and S. Klein, "Is the V-Form the Next Generation Organization? An Analysis of Challenges, Pitfalls and Remedies of ICT-Enabled Virtual Organizations Based on Social Capital Theory," *Journal of Information Technology* 23 (2008) 147–162.

H. Smith, "Universities, Innovation, and Territorial Development: A Review of the Evidence," *Environment and Planning C* 23:1 (2007) 98–141.

E. Wenger, *Communities of Practice: Learning, Meaning and Identity* (Cambridge: Cambridge University Press, 1998).

Index

Page numbers in **bold** type refer to figures
Page numbers in *italic* type refer to tables
Page numbers followed by 'n' refer to notes

Abreu, M.: et al 68
accessibility index: multi-modal 73, **73**
Allwinkle, S.: and Cruickshank, P. 1–14
Amin, A.: and Roberts, J. 18–19, 21, 36, 37n, 83–4
Amsterdam 2
architecture 42–6; enterprise 43; global overview **45**, **47**; information *see* information architecture; innovation 42; service-oriented 23, 46
Audi 55

Berry, C.R.: and Glaeser, E.L. 67
Budapest 55
Bush, V. 77
business models 39–42, *42*, 46–51; definition 41–2; FSP 11, 40; implementing 47; web-based 40

Calgary 57–8, **58**
capital 65–9, 83; human 67, 69, 75–6, **76**; intellectual 12; social 5–7, 96
Caragliu, A.: Del Bo, C. and Nijkamp, P. 12, 65–77; and Nijkamp, P. 68
Castells, M. 4
cities: creative 59, 61; intelligent 3, 8–10, 17; reinvention 53, 57, *see also* smart cities
Clark, K.B.: and Henderson, R.M. 42
class: creative 72, **72**
Cohen, W.: and Levinthal, D. 68
Cohendet, P.: and Simon, L. 58
community 5–6; natural 6
community grid for learning (CGfL) 7
community of practice (CoPs) 9–12, 17–37, 83–4, 90; characteristics *19*, 20–2, *22*, 36; co-designing on-line services 21; e-learning platform 20; eCitizenship module 27; ICT skills 27–8, **28**; innovation-seeking projects 19; interest groups 19; literature 18; meaning and purpose 36; monitoring and evaluating 21–2; netiquette 19; network 10; online interaction 19; shared enterprise 20–1

content management system (CMS) 91
Cooke, P.: and Leydesdorff, L. 55
Cooper, I.: Deakin, M. and Lombardi, P. 9–10, 17–37
Council for Mutual Economic Assistance (COMECON) 76
Creating Smart(er) Cities Conference (Edinburgh 2009) 1
creative city 59, 61
creative class 72, **72**
Cruickshank, P. 13, 83–98; and Allwinkle, S. 1–14
cybernetic mechanisms 61n

data: Urban Audit 12, 70, 72, 74, 77; USPTO 57–8, **58**
Deakin, M.: and Leydesdorff, L. 11–12, 53–61; Lombardi, P. and Cooper, I. 9–10, 17–37
Del Bo, C.: and Florio, M. 77n; Nijkamp, P. and Caragliu, A. 12, 65–77
digital library 30–1
Dublin 24, 59

e-commerce 41
e-government (e-Gov) services 10, 13–14, 17–18, 21–4, 30–6, 40–1, 47, 83–5, 91–3, 96; business models *42*; development 91; model 23; scenario 33–4, **35**, *36*; semantically interoperable 30; wealth **75**
e-learning 8, 24–5; benchmarking *25*; CoPs platform 20; ICT skills 27, **28**; intelligent solution 24–5; LMS 25–6; materials and courses 26–9, **26**; platform 20, 24–31, **31**; services 24
Eastern Europe 55
eCity platform 23, 30–3, **31**
Edinburgh 6–7, 24, 57–9, **58**; City Council Smart City Vision 2; Learning Partnership 7; Napier University 84
education: International Standard Classification of Education (ISCED) 75
enterprise architecture 43

INDEX

Epractice.eu 93, **95**, 96n
eTopia demonstrator 10, 22, 32–3; storylines 32–3; testing 32–3
Etzkowitz, H.: and Leydesdorff, L. 55, 85, 88
Europe: Eastern 55
European smart cities 65–77; GDP 70, 74; middle size 70; population 65–6, **66**; PPS 70, 74; public transportation 74, **74**; wealth 74–6, **74**
European Union (EU) 55, 67; Information Society Technologies Program 17; Sixth Framework Program 17; transition 55

Florida, R. 59, 68, 72; and Stolarick, K. 59
Florio, M.: and Del Bo, C. 77n
full-service provider (FSP) business model 11, 40

GDP (gross domestic product): European smart cities 70, 74
geographically intelligent settlements 6
Glaeser, E.L. 68; and Berry, C.R. 67
Glasgow 24, 58, **58**
Gothenburg 59
governments 39–41, 49; university-industry dynamic 53, *see also* e-government (e-Gov) services
Graham, S.: and Marvin, S. 4
Gupta, J.N.D.: and Sharma, S.K. 40

Halpern, D. 5–6
Helsinki 24
Henderson, R.M.: and Clark, K.B. 42
Hessels, L.: and Van Lente, H. 58
Hollands, R. 1, 2–5, 56, 67–9
human capital 67, 69, 75–6, **76**
Hungary 55

IBM 2
ICTs (information and communication technologies) 2, 3–4, 13, 65, 67, 77, 83; infrastructure 67; networks 6–7; skills 27–8, **28**
industry: university-government dynamic 53
information architecture 42–4, 46–8; back-end 44, 46, 48–9, 50–1; front-end 44, 48, 50–1; integration 50–1; sound 47; types 48, 50
infrastructure 4, 67–8; ICT 67; novel 2; soft 68
innovation: architecture 42; modular 42, 48; -seeking projects (CoPs) 19; systems 54–7
IntelCities 17–18, 90; CoPs 17–37; *see also* triple-helix model
intellectual capital 12
intellectual property: world organization (WIPO) 57–8, **58**

intelligent cities 3, 8–10, 17
Intelligent Community Forum 67
intelligent settlements: geographically 6
interest groups: CoPs 19
International Standard Classification of Education (ISCED) 75

Janssen, M.: *et al* 41; and Kuk, G. 10–11, 39–51
Jauhiainen, J.: and Suorsa, K. 85–6, **87**
Jensen, C.: and Tragardh, B. 85–6, **87**
Josefsson, U. 19

knowledge: -intensive policies 59; localized knowledge spillovers (LKS) 67
knowledge-management system (KMS) 29–30; Document Manager (DM) 29–30; toolkit 31
Komninos, N. 3, 11, 56
Krakow 74
Krippendorff, K. 61n
Kuk, G.: and Janssen, M. 10–11, 39–51

Landry, C. 11, 56
Layne, K.: and Lee, J. 40
learning *see* e-learning
Learning Management System (LMS) 25–6
Lee, J.: and Layne, K. 40
Levinthal, D.: and Cohen, W. 68
Leydesdorff, L.: and Cooke, P. 55; and Deakin, M. 11–12, 53–61; and Etzkowitz, H. 55, 85, 88
library: digital 30–1
Linthicum, D.S. 43
localized knowledge spillovers (LKS) 67
Lombardi, P.: Cooper, I. and Deakin, M. 9–10, 17–37

management systems: knowledge (KMS) 29–31; learning (LMS) 25–6
Manchester 2, 9, 17
Marvin, S.: and Graham, S. 4
Mayer, H. 76
MediaWiki 91
Mitchell, W. 4, 10, 22
Montreal 57–9, **58**, 60; growth 58
Müller, A.L. 59
multi-modal accessibility index 73, **73**
myEdinburgh.org 7; CGfL 7; information portal 7

neoclassical theories 75
Netherlands 39, 40–51
netiquette 19
networks 3, 6; CoPs 10
New Economic Geography 73

INDEX

Nijkamp, P.: and Caragliu, A. 68; Caragliu, A. and Del Bo, C. 12, 65–77
Nooteboom, B. 57

online interaction 19
Orr, J. 18
Oslo Manual (OECD and EUROSTAT) 67

people 4
Poelhekke, S. 68
population: European smart cities 65–6, **66**
public transportation: European smart cities 74, **74**
Purchasing Power Parity (PPP) 66, 77n
purchasing power standards (PPS) 70, 74

Rational Unified Process (RUP) 23
reconstruction 11
regeneration: urban 6–7
reinvention: cities 53, 57
Reykjavik 24
Roberts, J.: and Amin, A. 18–19, 21, 36, 37n, 83–4

Science Museum 65
self-congratulatory tone: smart cities 2, 3
Semantic Web 30
services: e-learning 24
Services Oriented Architecture (SOA) 4, 23
Shapiro, J.M. 73
Sharma, S.K.: and Gupta, J.N.D. 40
Siena 17
Simon, L.: and Cohendet, P. 58
smart card portal 5
smart cities 1–4, 8–9, **8**, 12, 39, 65–7, 83; city's claim 2–3; definition 1–4, 8–9, 66–7, 69–70; European *see* European smart cities; forerunners 1, 2; indicators 70, *71*; legacy 4; real 4; trends 83
Smart Cities partnership 13–14, 84, **85**, 86–8, 95
Smart Cities Regional Academic Network (SCRAN) 13–14, 83–98; CMS 91; fund 94–5; shared enterprise 90–1, **90**; technology 92; three-way partnership 84; wiki 91, **92**, **93**, **94**; work commissioning 94–5
Smart City programs 2
Smith, H. 85–6, **87**
social capital 5–7, 96
Social Inclusion Partnerships (SIPs) 6–7
socialization 4
Southampton 5

Stockholm 74
Stolarick, K.: and Florida, R. 59
structured query language (SQL) protocols 29
Suorsa, K.: and Jauhiainen, J. 85–6, **87**

technology 39, 56; Web 2.0 44–6, 48, 50, 96, *see also* ICTs
Tragardh, B.: and Jensen, C. 85–6, **87**
transportation: public 74, **74**
triple-helix model 11–14, 53–61, 83, 85–8, **87**, **89**; neo-evolutionary perspective 54, 59–61; overlay 55; reflections 60–1; studies 85; theory 56; university-industry-government dynamic 53

Unique Modeling Language (UML) 23
United Nations Educational, Scientific and Cultural Organization (UNESCO) 75
United States Patent and Trademark (USPTO) data 57–8, **58**
universities 55, 89–90; Edinburgh Napier 84; industry-government dynamic 53; Vienna Technology 70
Urban Audit data 12, 70, 72, 74, 77
urban growth 65
urban performance 65
urban regeneration 6–7

Van Lente, H.: and Hessels, L. 58
Vienna University of Technology 70
Vitale, M.: and Weill, P. 41

wealth 74–6, **74**; creation 12; e-government 75; European smart cities 74–6, **74**
Web 2.0 technologies 44–6, 48, 50, 96
web-based business models 40
websites 41; design 41; monitors 41; Smart City Thinking 2
Weill, P.: and Vitale, M. 41
Wenger, E. 18, 83
Will the Real Smart City Please Stand Up? (Hollands) 2
World Intellectual Property Organization (WIPO) data 57–8, **58**
www.smartcitythinking.com 2

Zachman, J.A. 43